A Kennel Club Guide to

DOG DAYS OUT!

PUBLISHED BY

The Kennel Club

A Kennel Club Guide to

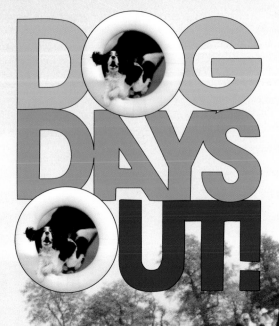

DOG DAYS OUT!

Laura Colborn

Credits

Author
Laura Colborn
Designer/Art Director
Phil Gorton
Project Manager
for The Kennel Club
Kathryn Symns
Production Co-ordinator
for Kingdom Books
Dave Downing
Digital Pre-press
Ace Graphics, London
Printed & Bound
in Singapore by
Tien Wah Press

Original Commissioned
pictures in the Dog Clubs,
Shows and Showing,
Obedience Competitions,
Agility and Working Trials
Chapters are the Copyright
of The Kennel Club
Special Photographer
Mary Wadsworth

The Kennel Club would like
to thank the following
photographers whose work
also appears and who
retain their own Copyright:
Christian Guildford
Peter Heard
Marc Henrie
P.E. Rawlings
Sharkey
Steve Tanner
Mary Wadsworth
Derek Whitehouse
R.Willbie

The Author would like to
thank the management
and members of
Earlsfield and District
Dog Training Club and the
management, members
and competitors at the
Southern Alsatian Training
Society for allowing us to
take photographs of them
in action and for making
us feel so welcome.
Thanks also to Charles
Colborn for his invaluable
editorial advice.

Contents

Dog Days Out!

First published in 2000 by
The Kennel Club,
1-5, Clarges Street,
Piccadilly, London W1Y 8AB.

In association with Kingdom Books.
GB-096

ISBN 185279 174-8

You and Your Dog

You've read all the books and chosen the right dog for your family and lifestyle. You've taken the time to find a reputable breeder with puppies available and picked out the dog you really want. Now, you've finally got your new canine companion home and can start to enjoy life with him.

You can have so much fun with a dog; training him, playing with him in the garden or local park, going for long country rambles, or a quick stroll down to the shops, or simply enjoying a cosy night in with the family. But did you know that there are literally thousands of events held every year offering you a whole range of great, fun days out with your dog?

Open the door to an exciting new world of hobbies with your dog.

Every week, up and down the country, there are dog owners, just like you, taking part in all sorts of fun and fascinating hobbies with their dogs. If you have just bought a dog, or have owned a dog for some time and never known that there is so much more you could be enjoying, this book provides an introduction to this new and exciting 'dog world'.

We'll be looking at vital information for new dog owners and giving details of a whole range of rewarding canine events and activities. From dog shows to agility competitions, whether your dog is a pet pooch, or a pampered pedigree, The Kennel Club organises something for everyone to enjoy.

Whether you walk away with a prize or not...

The Kennel Club

The Kennel Club is the governing body of the 'dog world' in this country. The first of its kind in the world, it was set up in 1873 to regulate the many dog shows and other competitions that were springing up all over the country at the time, and to create a definitive list of pedigree dog names to put a stop to the confusion and 'sharp practices' that were widespread.

The Kennel Club has come a long way since then to become a well respected, successful organisation, with the welfare of dogs and dog owners very much at its heart. The initial list of pedigree names started in 1873 is now a huge computer database listing over 4,000,000 dogs. All of these dogs are eligible to compete at Kennel Club events and nearly 7,000 canine competitions, from the grandest dog show of them all, Crufts, to the humblest charity show held as part of the village fete, are licensed by The Kennel Club each year. Over 2000 canine clubs and societies are also registered with, and governed by, The Kennel Club, catering for every breed and every interest in the world of dogs.

There are over 140 staff at The Kennel Club's offices in London and Aylesbury, working hard to organise this wealth of information, events and services. The Kennel Club is actually governed by an elected Committee, chosen from The Kennel Club's membership of 750, and it is the staff's job to put the Committee's decisions into practice. The Kennel Club Yearbook reflects all the Committee's decisions and details all the rules and regulations governing everything, from registering your dog, to setting up a dog club.

Most people know of The Kennel Club as the organisers of Crufts. The Kennel Club has organised Crufts since 1948 and every year thousands of people, both at the show and watching on television, are able to see the very finest examples of dogs in this country competing against each other for the ultimate of prizes.

In 1994 an exciting new innovation, called Discover Dogs, made its first appearance at Crufts. The aim was to gather together examples of every breed so that members of the public could learn all about the choice, care and training of different breeds of dog, from the experts. Such was its success that it has continued at Crufts every year and is now an event in its own right, held annually in London.

...there's so much to see and do at Crufts that you are sure to feel like a winner.

How We Can Help You

This book will be describing in detail, Kennel Club licensed activities in this country, but The Kennel Club organises so many more things to make a dog owner's life easier, that also deserve a mention.

As well as registering dogs and organising and overseeing all aspects of canine competitions in this country, The Kennel Club's aim of promoting the improvement and welfare of dogs has also led to the development of a range of useful goods and services for dog owners and breeders. New dog owners in particular are well catered for, with services designed to take the worry out of adding a new canine member to the family.

Petlog

Hundreds of dogs and other pets go missing from home every year. The Kennel Club is well aware of the distress and heartbreak this can cause and, together with the RSPCA and the Scottish SPCA, has set up the hugely successful Petlog National Pet Identification Scheme. Over 7,000,000 dogs have been added to the national Petlog database since 1995, making the scheme the most successful in the country and the main source of reference for local authorities, police and established welfare and rescue organisations.

There are 3 methods of canine identification; a tattoo on the inside of the ear, or leg, a microchip, or a simple collar tag. As tattoos can fade and collar tags become lost, microchipping is now considered the best method of identifying your pet - it's safe, permanent and effective. Your vet can tell you all about the procedure and microchipping your pet provides automatic inclusion, for life, on the Petlog database, free of charge.

Once your pet is registered with Petlog you will receive a collar tag with its unique Petlog identification number as well as a registration certificate and, most importantly, peace of mind if your pet should stray from home. If you want to find out more about this scheme contact The Kennel Club on 0870 6066751.

Kennel Gazette keeps you up to date with all that's important in the world of dogs.

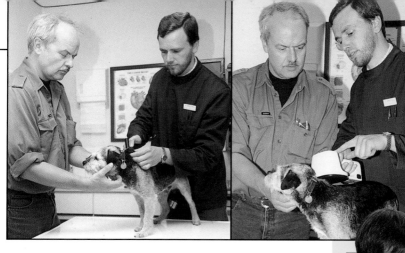

Pet Insurance

Owning a dog is a great source of pride and pleasure, but it can also cause great anxiety and expense if illness, or injury, should arise. Part of responsible dog ownership is being prepared for problems should they occur, and Pet Protect Insurance is ,therefore, offering the owners of Kennel Club registered dogs, protection against the rising cost of veterinary treatment.

If you want to keep your dog in the peak of condition without cutting costs, comprehensive insurance cover, such as offered by this scheme, may solve your problems. For further details and an application form, contact the staff at Pet Protect on 01372 848028.

Canine Code

As part of The Kennel Club's continuing educational programme of responsible dog ownership, a booklet called The Canine Code is available, free of charge, to anybody who cares about dogs and their place in society. The Canine Code gives valuable advice to prospective dog owners, as well as listing some essential 'do's' and 'don'ts' to help you develop a rewarding relationship with your dog.

Kennel Gazette

This informative and colourful magazine is packed with interesting articles about all things 'doggy'. It's also full of information about what events are being held around the country and explanations of Kennel Club rules and regulations. There are plenty of magazines about dogs for sale, but this magazine is the only one produced by The Kennel Club. To take out a subscription, phone The Kennel Club on 0870 6066750 and ask for the Publications Department.

Having your dog microchipped will help you to be re-united if you are ever parted from your precious pet.

Library

The Kennel Club boasts the largest canine reference library in Europe and it is open to the public by appointment. You can trace the history of your favourite breed, or simply read up on all those things you've always wanted to know about our canine friends. For more information contact the Library on 020 7518 1009.

The Kennel Club Charitable Trust
(Registered Charity Number 327802)

The Kennel Club's Charitable Trust co-ordinates individual charitable donations and funds from The Kennel Club to benefit the canine world. The Trust aims to improve educational and scientific advancement through research into canine diseases, to promote dogs as therapeutic and practical aids to humans and to relieve the suffering of dogs who are in need of care and attention. Since its inception in 1989, grants totalling £700,000 have been made to the benefit of dogs in this country.

Rescue Directory

Unfortunately, some dogs find themselves in need of new homes when their owners' personal circumstances change and they can no longer look after them. There are also thoughtless and cruel people who simply abandon dogs and puppies when they become bored with them. A network of rescue organisations and charities throughout the country takes in such dogs and tries to find new, loving homes for them. The Kennel Club Rescue Directory lists hundreds of rescue organisations, from big charities like the National Canine Defence League, to small specialised organisations dealing with only one breed of dog. The Directory is sent to all local authorities, police forces and veterinary services to help make sure that no dog misses the chance to be re-homed. If you want to give an unwanted dog a new home contact The Kennel Club for the details of those people who can help you.

Puppy Packs

The Kennel Club is inundated every day with people enquiring where they can find puppies of a particular breed. The Kennel Club responds to these requests by sending out a list of breeders who have puppies for sale in the near future and, where none are available, the contact details of clubs whose members may also have puppies for sale. These 'puppy packs' also include the useful and educational leaflet The Canine Code and other information that first time dog owners will find useful.

Staff and Helplines

No matter what your problem The Kennel Club staff will do their best to sort it out for you quickly and efficiently. You can help the staff help you, by addressing your queries to the right section. The main contact telephone numbers are:-

Are you ready to look after a dog? The Canine Code spells out the do's and don'ts of responsible dog ownership...

...get it right and your dog will be jumping for joy.

Main switchboard	0870 6066750
Insurance	01372 848 028
Library	020 7518 1009
Good Citizen Dog Scheme	020 7518 1011
General Fax number	020 7518 1058

Registering Your Dog

Before you get involved with any Kennel Club licensed activity you must ensure that your dog is properly registered with The Kennel Club. The vast majority of dogs registered with The Kennel Club are pure-bred dogs, but non-pedigree dogs will be accepted to allow them to take part in competitions, such as Agility and Flyball.

Dealing first with pure-bred dogs, there are over 195 breeds currently eligible for registration with The Kennel Club. The breeds are categorised in Groups according to the origin of the breed: the seven Groups are Hound, Gundog, Terrier, Utility, Working, Pastoral and Toy.

Only the breeder of a litter can apply to The Kennel Club to register puppies. When the puppies are sold, the breeder of the litter should provide the new owner with The Kennel Club registration certificate, with their part of the transfer section completed. The new owner must then complete their section of the transfer and return it to The Kennel Club, for the dog to be officially registered in their name. It is only once this has been done that the new owner can start to take part in Kennel Club licensed activities.

If you are completely new to the world of pure-bred dogs the forms can look a little complicated, but if you have any queries, The Kennel Club staff are always more than happy to guide you through the procedure.

It is very important to remember that your dog will be registered with The Kennel Club under the name that appears on your certificate. Your dog may be 'Ben' or 'Rufus' to you, but in all communications with The Kennel Club you will have to refer to him by his full, registered name and registration number.

If you are going to take part in competitions with your dog, not only must you make sure that your dog's exact registered name appears on the entry form, but that all other details have been completed properly.

If you own a cross-bred dog you can still take part in most Kennel Club licensed events, but you must register your dog with The Kennel Club first. You won't be able to enter Field Trials or the world of canine beauty Shows, as they are exclusively for pure-bred dogs, but you can still have great fun with your dog by getting involved with the sports of Obedience, Agility, Flyball and Working Trials, which are explained in detail later in this book. It is a much simpler process to register your dog with The Kennel Club for these sorts of competitions. Remember though, that you will still need to refer to your dog's Kennel Club registered name every time you contact The Kennel Club, or enter any competitions.

To get more details and an application form to add your dog's name to The Kennel Club Working Trial and Obedience Register, telephone 0870 6066750.

Your dog may be good old Rufus to you, but remember that if he is Kennel Club registered he will have a much grander name, which you must use whenever you enter him for competitions, or write to The KC.

First Steps

Probably the first person who will be able to give you advice about your dog is the breeder of the litter. They will be able to give you advice, not only about how best to care for your new dog, but also, what sort or things your dog may be suited to getting involved with. If your dog comes from 'Show' stock, the breeder may well tell you all about dog shows and how to get started; if you have bought a gundog your breeder may be able to tell you how to train your dog to enter Field Trials; if your breeder is an Agility enthusiast they might be able to tell you where your nearest Agility club is. No matter what aspect of competition your breeder is interested in, if at all, there really is no substitute for talking to someone who knows the breed well.

If you and your dog are going to be able to enjoy any form of competition you must take the time to find out about the nature of the event, train together and build up a real partnership. You will not only perform better in competition, but you will create a really rewarding relationship with your dog. There is no easy way to accomplish this and, no matter how experienced someone may be in the world of dogs, owning a new dog means starting at the very beginning.

Whether you want to go into competitions with your dog or not, a well-trained, obedient dog is a real credit to you. To help you towards this goal The Kennel Club has set up a unique, nationwide dog training scheme, called the Good Citizen Dog Scheme.

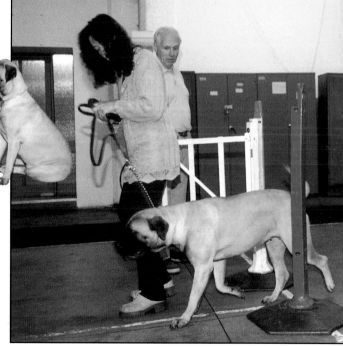

You know how excited dogs can be to get out for their walks – but imagine how dangerous it could be if they rushed out of the house and into traffic. The GCDS will teach your dog good door policy.

Good Citizen Dog Scheme

The first thing any new dog owner has to think about is how to transform their mischievous and playful puppy into a responsible and well behaved companion who won't get you, or himself, into trouble. With just this in mind The Kennel Club established the Good Citizen Dog Scheme in 1992. The scheme is the most successful dog training scheme in the country and some 30,000 dogs have taken part.

The Scheme aims to give basic training in those vital areas that transform a dog into a model canine citizen. Experienced dog trainers are on hand at the classes to tackle all those difficult training problems and can give you the benefit of many year's experience and involvement with dogs and dog training. You will have the opportunity of chatting to other dog owners in the class and seeing how their canine charges measure up to your dog. This really is the best introduction to the 'dog world' and will give you a taste of what a sociable and enjoyable time you can have with your dog.

It is open to everyone regardless of age, and all dogs whether pedigree or cross-breed, registered with The Kennel Club, or not. The courses take place over a number of weeks and cover basic exercises such as:

Leading the way! He may struggle at first but wearing a collar and lead will ensure his safety.

- Training your dog to accept a collar and lead.
- Training your dog to walk on a lead.
- Training your dog to walk on a lead without becoming distracted by people, or other dogs.
- Teaching your dog to lie down and stay on command.
- Grooming.
- Ensuring that you, the owner, have some form of 'poop scoop' to clear up after your dog, at all times.
- Teaching your dog to allow you to examine its teeth and mouth, eyes, feet and ears.
- Training your dog to return to you when called.

You and your dog will have to face a test at the end of the course and, if you are successful, you'll be rewarded with a certificate, a rosette and, above all, a well-behaved pet. If you have enjoyed mastering the basic training course, you can go on to take courses at Silver and Gold stages, where you can add to your experience and knowledge.

Over 880 clubs and local authorities run these courses and, if you would like more details, just give The Kennel Club a ring on 020 7518 1011 to find out where the course closest to you is being held.

THE KENNEL CLUB

A Video Guide to the

Good Citizen Dog Scheme

Does your dog pass the test?

Produced by The Kennel Club

A Video Guide

You can also view an enjoyable and educational video which explains all about the Good Citizen Dog Scheme, entitled *Does your dog pass the test?* This video is available by sending a cheque or postal order, for £5.99 to The Kennel Club, or by contacting the Publications Department with your credit card details.

Dog Clubs

Training Clubs

Once you and your dog have mastered basic good behaviour, you are ready to look at taking things a step further. Again there is plenty of professional help available to set you on your way.

If you have taken part in the Good Citizen Dog Scheme you may well have gone to classes at your local dog training club and they can also help you and your dog progress beyond basic obedience. All sorts of things will be taught from walking to heel, sitting and staying on command, or more specialist training for competition such as scent, retrieve, send-away and down-stay exercises.

It is well worth joining your local training club as there is usually an active social life, with all sorts of competitions and information available to all. You will find out all manner of useful information about dogs - where and when shows and competitions are going to be held, what's involved with the different types of competition and, where to go locally for such things as veterinary services, or, the best grooming parlour.

Clubs may also hold Obedience matches, which are knockout competitions within a club's membership or between two or three clubs. All sorts of prize cards and rosettes may be available and these fun evenings may very well be your first experience of competition.

You may also find that your local training club runs more formal competitions for Obedience, Agility, Flyball and Working Trials. Going along and spectating at these competitions is the only way to find out if these activities are really for you and your dog or not. If you do decide that you want to get involved in, say, Agility, remember that you will probably have to do a lot more hard work and training to succeed in

Training nights at your local club are great fun – and your dog will love the classes too!

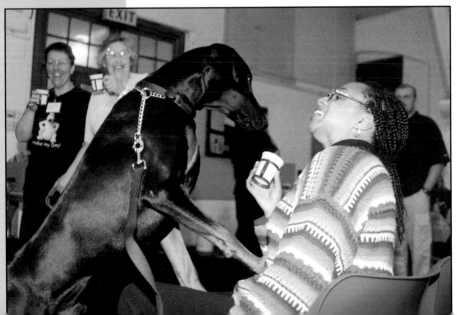

competition, but it will be worth it for the sheer enjoyment.

It is also worth remembering that clubs don't run themselves and hard pressed organisers may be very grateful for any offers of help.

The Kennel Club keeps a full list of dog training clubs located throughout the country and to find out your nearest club simply give them a call on 0870 6066750.

Ringcraft Clubs

The most popular form of canine competition in this country is the dog show - the formal 'beauty contests' for pure-bred dogs, such as can be seen at Crufts. The Kennel Club has set a 'Breed Standard' for every breed of dog, which represents the ideal conformation and characteristics for that breed. At shows, the Judge must compare each dog with the Breed Standard to find the dog nearest to that ideal picture of the breed.

If you know that you are going to want to develop your dog into a 'show' dog, there are many clubs specialising in 'ringcraft'. Ringcraft classes teach you how to prepare and present your dog so that he looks his best for the judge in the show ring. A great deal of time and effort goes into presenting a dog for exhibition at a show and even getting your dog to perform in the ring is a lot harder than it looks. The judge will not be impressed by a dog that only wants to slouch in the corner, or amble around the ring ungracefully. It is very important that you learn how to present your dog in the show ring to show off all his finer points.

This can all be pretty difficult to achieve; the dog has got to want to show off for his owner and a good deal of time and effort has to go into building teamwork. Luckily, the people who run ringcraft clubs have a great deal of experience in the 'show scene' and will be able to reveal all the techniques and tricks of the trade.

The experts will be on hand to provide plenty of friendly advice and guidance.

The GCDS teaches that meeting and coping with other dogs and people is an important first step to obedience.

Ringcraft clubs will also have a copy of the Breed Standard for your breed so that you can see how closely your dog measures up to perfection.

The Kennel Club can help you with the details of your nearest ringcraft club if you telephone 0870 6066750.

Other Clubs

Starting out with the Good Citizen Dog Scheme and your local training club or ringcraft club, really is the best possible introduction to the world of dogs. Through them, you and your dog will learn good basic obedience, you'll find out about, and perhaps attend, some events and start to learn about actually taking part in the canine competition that most appeals to you, as well as being able to learn about Kennel Club rules and regulations from more seasoned dog folk.

However, before you can start to enter competitions you need to know a little more about the way the world of dogs is structured and all the other sorts of clubs that exist.

The Kennel Club licenses over 7000 canine events every year, but the management of all these events lies in the hands of the 2000 or so dog clubs in Britain. These dog clubs were all set up by enthusiasts and some have been in existence as long as The Kennel Club itself. There are several categories of clubs all catering for people with different interests.

Kennel Club regulations require clubs to have properly formulated constitutions which lay down the ground rules as to how they will be run and, of course, clubs and dog shows need a dedicated management team if they are to work at all.

Clubs are run by elected committees which include a number of officers with specific functions and duties. Typically, the chairman will be responsible for overseeing the business of the club and conducting committee meetings; the club secretary will be in charge of the club's administration and correspondence and must carry out the decisions of the rest of the committee; the treasurer is responsible for seeing that the club's accounts are kept in good order. There may be other committee members with specific duties such as the show manager who takes charge of all practical arrangements for shows, or a welfare officer who co-ordinates rescue and re-homing for their particular breed, or area. The committee structure varies from club to club but, if you want to join a club, the best person to speak to, in the first instance, is the club secretary.

Breed Clubs

There are over 195 breeds of dog recognised by The Kennel Club and almost every one of these breeds has at least one breed club. More unusual breeds, such as the Alaskan Malamute, have only one club, but a really popular breed, like the Cocker Spaniel, boasts 24 clubs distributed across the entire country.

The people who set up and belong to these clubs are breed enthusiasts; they may have been involved with a particular breed all their lives, or be keen newcomers. As these clubs are for breed enthusiasts, they will be involved with all sorts

Your club may also sell all those essential treats and snacks your dog can't do without!

Not to put too fine a point on it – the help and advice you will receive at your local club are vital to happy dog ownership.

of activities which promote the well being and understanding of their particular breed. Seminars and classes may be organised to discuss nutrition, grooming and showing techniques, the history of the breed, or perhaps to address hereditary problems in the breed. Judging seminars may be organised to give would-be judges a greater insight into the breed and lists of judges will be compiled. Clubs also produce magazines and other publications and dog shows may be scheduled.

Breed clubs can generally hold 2, or 3, shows a year and

Making a day of it – dog shows and competitions can attract quite a crowd.

they are real high spots in the club's year. They represent a chance for fellow enthusiasts to get together for a day's competition and provide a great opportunity to socialise. Of course there is inevitably some healthy rivalry, as there would be in any hobby, and some people are never happy unless they walk away with a first prize. Most people, however, are there to show their dog, have a good day out and see plenty of fine examples of the breed they love.

Clubs can also hold up to 12 Breed Matches a year. Breed matches, like Obedience matches, are knockout competitions for club members. They represent another good opportunity for club members to meet socially and see how each other's dogs are developing as 'Show' animals by competing in these friendly competitions and winning prize cards and rosettes

Sub-Group and Group Societies

A Sub-Group is a categorisation of dogs that incorporates more than one related breed. For example, the development and historic function of Pointers and Setters, as breeds, is similar, so there is a club that looks after the interests of these breeds as a unit, existing alongside all the separate clubs for the various types of Pointer and Setter.

Similarly, there are societies that cater for those people who are enthusiastic about a whole group of dogs, say, for example, Terriers. These are known as Group societies.

Sub-Group and Group societies are similar in function and design to breed societies and they also schedule seminars and shows.

General Canine Societies

As well as societies dedicated to specific breeds there are hundreds of clubs catering for dog lovers on a regional basis.

Whereas breed clubs see themselves as promoting the well being and reputation of a particular breed, general canine societies are geared towards more general interests and to scheduling shows. These shows provide a valuable testing ground for new exhibitors and their dogs as well as new judges and other competition officials.

This does not mean that your local general canine society will not organise all sorts of other activities. They too may schedule lectures on welfare, grooming and showing, organise social activities, run training and ringcraft sessions and hold matches as well.

The larger general canine societies run the prestigious All Breed Championship Shows which attract thousands of competitors every year. As well as being top competitions with many prizes and awards on offer, these shows are major exhibitions as well, with trade stands selling all sorts of dog paraphernalia, visitors attending from far and wide, and hundreds of spectators.

Agricultural Societies and Municipal Authorities

This is a relatively small category of societies, which stage dog shows only as part of, say, a large agricultural exhibition such as North Devon Agricultural Show, or as part of a city's exhibition day, such as that put on by Hull City Council. They do not tend to offer any of the training or social aspects of other types of club but can be relied upon to schedule interesting competitions once a year that may attract competitors from quite a distance.

Specialist Societies

All the clubs we have spoken about in this section so far have been geared towards the beauty side of canine competition. There are also hundreds of clubs set up specifically to cater for the sports of Obedience, Agility and Flyball, Working Trials, and Field Trials and Gundog Working Tests.

You and your dog may well have become involved in the world of canine competition by going along to your local training club and these tend also to be the clubs dedicated, at a higher level, to Obedience, Working Trials, Agility and Flyball. This book will be looking at all these fascinating sports, as well as Field Trials and Gundog Working Tests, in more detail later on.

From small breed club shows to large agricultural fairs there's bound to be something that catches your eye.

Shows and Showing

You've been going to ringcraft classes for some time and perhaps been involved in some matches at your local club. You've learnt all about how to prepare your dog for exhibition, you understand the Breed Standard and ringcraft classes have taught you what will happen during judging in the show ring. Now you and your dog are ready to compete at a fully fledged dog show, and perhaps even start to win some prizes.

What's on, Where and When?

You may find out about forthcoming shows through friends, or through seeing a show advertised at your local club. This is a good place to start as, not only will more experienced people be on hand at the club to tell you whether it would be suitable for you and your dog to attend, but you may also have the chance of entering the show with a friend so that you can learn the ropes together.

There are other ways of finding out what's on, when and where. The Kennel Gazette contains a Show Guide which lists the details of all the up and coming events and there are two weekly newspapers called 'Dog World' and 'Our Dogs', which can be ordered through newsagents, which also carry details. As The Kennel Club licenses every dog show, the Show Diary Section at The Kennel Club's offices can also tell you what shows are scheduled to take place.

Shows are held all year round, though most shows are held during the summer months to take advantage of the, hopefully, good weather. Shows also tend to be held at weekends, to give as many people as possible the chance of entering. The Kennel Club tries to ensure that clubs do not hold shows in the same area on the same day, so that there is a good choice of shows spread throughout the country every week.

Types of Show

The number of categories and grades of dog shows can be bewildering for anyone new to dog showing. There is a lot of jargon used to categorise shows which can all be pretty confusing to newcomers.

The first question you should ask yourself is whether you want to enter a single breed show, or a general multi-breed show.

Single breed shows, as the name suggests, have classes for just one breed of dog and are organised by a breed club. Such shows are likely to attract breed specialists who may have been involved in the breeding and showing of a particular breed for many years and, as such, can provide you with an opportunity to really learn about your breed from the experts. The club show may be the main event of the club's year so there could be a large entry of keen and experienced competitors with plenty of specialist classes scheduled.

Some people prefer to start out on their show career by entering general shows that schedule classes for several breeds of dog. These shows are run by general canine

One day the crowds could be applauding your wins in the show ring.

societies and are a good testing ground for new exhibitors and judges. As the show will not be run by a specialist breed club there will not be a huge selection of classes for each breed and some breeds may not even have their own classes, but will be all in together in a Variety Class (more of which later). As there are many more general canine societies than there are breed clubs, there are always plenty of these shows held every year.

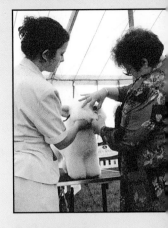

Has your dog got what it takes to impress the judge and become a winner?

Grades of Show

Within these two broad categories of breed shows and general shows, shows are further broken down into restricted and non-restricted shows.

Restricted Shows

This category of show is limited either to the members of the club holding the show, or limited to exhibitors from a particular area.

There will be a wide range of classes scheduled. As this is the lowest grade of show, the top winning dogs are not permitted to enter. This allows the less experienced dogs and owners to develop their showing technique, and have a chance of winning an award card and rosette or two. Shows at this level tend to be informal and relaxed, social occasions although of course there will be some friendly rivalry and competition.

Benching, common at larger shows, can be a real home from home for you and your dogs.

Non-restricted Shows

There are two types of shows that are open to everyone, 'Open Shows' and 'Championship Shows'.

Open Shows are just that - anyone can enter, from anywhere in the country, and it doesn't matter what awards a dog may have won before, as long as it is entered in the correct class. These shows are very popular and can attract many hundreds of competitors.

Championship Shows are the most prestigious shows where Kennel Club Challenge Certificates (also known as CC's, or tickets, in the show scene) are on offer. Challenge Certificates are the very highest award a dog can gain and they are awarded only to the very best dogs each year. If a dog wins three Challenge Certificates it is entitled to be known as a Champion. The Kennel Club only allows certain clubs to run Championship Shows and it is only by competing in these shows that you can win The Kennel Club's top award.

Benched or Unbenched

A further categorisation is whether a show is benched or unbenched. Benching does not mean, as many people new to dog showing have thought before, that there will be seats available for you to watch the judging! Benches are rows of raised compartments, or stalls, that your dog must be kept on at all times when he is not being judged or exercised. There are rings at the back of each bench to which you can clip your dog's chain, or lead, for security. If your dog travels in a cage you can keep your dog in its cage on the bench. Most smaller shows don't have benching but The Kennel Club insists that there is benching at larger shows for safety reasons.

Usually, benching is allocated alphabetically by surname so that the exhibitors for each breed will be benched together, in order of their surnames. This makes it much easier to track down friends and, if you become a regular show-goer, you will soon get to know the people and dogs who are benched around you whenever you go to shows.

Competition Structure

There is another categorisation applied to shows in conjunction with all these others, and that is the competition structure of the show. The competition structure can be very complex as there are many different ways of organising the classes in a show. As this book is for new-comers to the show scene it is going to look only at the most common types of dog show. The more complicated and unusual types of show will be looked at in detail in another Kennel Club Guide.

How to Enter a Show

So you should now be able to tell one sort of show from another. If you see an Unbenched Fox Terrier Club Limited Show advertised you know that its a show only for members of the Fox Terrier Club and that you will keep your dog by your side at the show; if you see the Chelmsford and District Canine Society Benched Open Show advertised you know that anyone can enter who chooses to do so and that there will be long lines of benches for all those dogs taking part.

Schedules

Once you have identified the show you want to take part in you must get hold of a copy of the schedule. All societies must issue a schedule some time before the show is to take place so that exhibitors can choose which classes they want to enter and find out all the other details about the show, like who will be judging, and where the show will take place. Schedules are often distributed to local clubs, but if you have seen a show advertised that you would like to enter, it's simply a question of phoning the club secretary for a schedule and entry form. The secretary may well ask you to send a stamped addressed envelope to keep the club's costs down.

Schedules can look quite daunting at first glance, particularly the ones for larger, multi-breed shows, which seem to be packed with information. However, all schedules contain the same basic information and once you have found your way round one of them it won't be too difficult in the future.

The front of the schedule will tell you the name of the society holding the show, what type of show it is, when and where it is to be held, who the club officials are and when the closing date is for completed entry forms. The rules and regulations governing that particular type of show must also appear in the schedule.

The schedule will then list all the classes being held at the show. If it is a single breed show this will be quite easy to follow. The classes are usually split into the same number of classes for dogs and classes for bitches.

The judge will scrutinise your dog's conformation and movement in the quest to find the dog closest to the Breed Standard.

The schedules for multi-breed shows are a little more complex and will list the classes for each breed. You simply find your breed of dog and look at the classes listed. With over 195 breeds of registered dog, societies very rarely provide classes for every single breed. If your breed of dog isn't listed there will be classes listed under 'Any Variety Not Separately Classified' (AVNSC) for each of the seven Groups of dogs. If you enter an AVNSC class you will be competing against a number of other breeds of dog from your Group.

Multi-breed shows may also list Variety classes, also known as Stakes classes, as well as the main breed and AVNSC classes. Such classes do not form part of the competition structure leading to the overall winner of the show, called Best in Show, but they do represent another chance to compete, and perhaps to win a prize or two. These classes will appear towards the back of the schedule.

Classes

Once you have found your way to the right part of the schedule you must select which class, or classes, you would like to enter. Open shows can schedule over 20 classes for each breed and, with detailed definitions for each class, it can all be rather confusing.

As a new exhibitor you will be interested in the beginners' classes which are either restricted to dogs of a certain age, or limited by the number of first prizes your dog may have won.

Age Restricted Classes

Minor Puppy, Puppy and Junior are all classes restricted to dogs of certain ages. No dogs may compete at Kennel Club licensed events until they are at least 6 months of age on the first day of the show. If your puppy is registered as being born on 1.1.97 he will not be eligible to enter shows until 1.7.97. If it is a two day show, and your breed is scheduled on the second day, your puppy can only take part if he was six months old on the first day of the show, rather than the day he is to compete. To calculate your puppy's upper age limit you can see that a dog born on 1.1.97 will come out of Minor Puppy for shows which start on, or after, 2.10.97, and out of Junior for all shows which start on, or after, 2.7.98.

Minor Puppy - For dogs of 6 and not exceeding 9 calendar months of age on the first day of the show.

Puppy - For dogs of 6 and not exceeding 12 calendar months of age on the first day of the show.

Junior - For dogs of 6 and not exceeding 18 calendar months on the first day of the show.

Qualification Restricted Classes

There are many other classes which can be scheduled which will be restricted by the awards your dog has gained in previous shows. The awards which should be counted towards qualifying for the various classes will differ depending on whether you enter a Limited show, or whether you enter an Open or Championship show.

Schedules will carry a full definition of each class so there is no need to memorise all the complicated qualifications.

All dogs can enter the Open class regardless of age or

No matter how big or small the show, and whatever your breed, there will be a class that's right for you.

previous wins, and many show societies might just put on a puppy class and an open class for each breed particularly if it is a small show.

It is also worth mentioning that you are not limited to just one class - you can enter as many classes as your dog is eligible for, and that you wish to compete in.

Entry Forms

Once you have deliberated over the schedule and chosen which class, or classes, you would like to compete in, you must complete the entry form accurately and legibly. The entry form will ask you for your dog's details. What breed he is, what his name is, his date of birth, his dam and his sire and the name of the person who bred him. It is vital that you give your dog's Kennel Club registered name and details, as errors may mean that you forfeit any prizes that you have won. If your dog's paperwork transferring him from the breeder's name to your name is still being processed by The Kennel Club you must put the letters T.A.F (Transfer Applied For) after his name.

You should also take care to fill in your name and address accurately or the show secretary could have problems in sending out any passes you will need for the show.

The class you wish to enter will be referred to by a number in the schedule and usually by an abbreviation of the class name. For example, PD will mean Puppy Dog and JB will mean Junior Bitch. There will be a full list of any abbreviations used in the schedule. You should clearly mark on the entry form which number class you would like to enter. It is well worth checking, and double checking, that you have written the correct class number down on the entry form, as mistakes can cause all sorts of problems on the day of the show, both for you, and the show organisers. Double check that you have selected the classes for the right breed of dog; if the classes have been split by sex that you have chosen the correct sex; and don't forget to sign the entry form!

Signing the entry form is important as it forms the contract between you and the show society. If the dog is jointly owned, both parties should sign the entry form unless one of the parties has the express written permission of the other to sign on their behalf. By signing, you are declaring that your dog is fit and healthy to take part in the show, that you will abide by Kennel Club rules and regulations, and that you will take part in all the classes you have entered if you attend the show. This is essential to the management of the show and for the sport in general.

As well as paying for each class you enter, the entry form may also give you the opportunity to pay for things like car parking and catalogues in advance, so make sure you write your cheque for the correct amount. Receiving the wrong fee is the problem show organisers face most commonly when dealing with entries. Once you have included the correct entry fee it is simply a question of posting the completed form back to the show secretary. You should do this within plenty of time of the closing date for entries. It is also recommended that you obtain a Certificate of Posting, from

A Certificate of Posting will ensure that you don't spend your day as a spectator rather than a competitor.

the Post Office. It can be terribly disappointing to travel all the way to a show to find that the show secretary never received your entry form. If, however, you take the time to obtain a Certificate of Posting, available free of charge from the Post Office, the show secretary will be able to accept your entry on the day of the show, although The Kennel Club will still have to look over everything after the show to check that all was in order. When completing a 'Proof of Posting' slip at the Post Office make sure that you clearly write the name of the show society and the words 'entry form'. The number of items being sent should be written in words and not numerals if it is to be considered valid. This may all seem a bit complicated for just sending off an entry form, but, after all, it's better to be safe than sorry!

Some show societies ask that you include a stamped addressed envelope so that ring cards and other passes for the show can be sent out in advance. At smaller shows you won't receive any information in advance of the show, so if you have any queries you should contact the show organisers.

At larger shows, when the show secretary has processed your entry form, you will be sent all the information you need to take part in the show. You should receive your ring number and any car park passes and catalogue vouchers. Your ring number is the number with which your dog will be identified, when being judged, as the judge is not allowed to know the names of those he is going to judge. This number will also be the number your dog is benched under if you are entering a benched show. If you are expecting to receive passes before the show and don't receive anything you should contact the show secretary.

Don't forget those creature comforts when planning your day's ringside viewing.

Your Day at a Show

Preparation

There is so much to think about before going to a show.

First of all there's your dog to consider. Dog shows are, after all, beauty shows so make sure your dog is going to look his best - he should be bathed, groomed and clipped, his teeth and ears should be clean and he should be in tip-top condition. Don't forget all the things you will need at the show - collar and lead, water bowl, food, benching chain, grooming kit. Does your dog have a favourite blanket or toy he likes to have with him when he travels or goes out?

You also need to think about your clothing. This may not seem the most obvious thing to think about when going to a dog show, yet it can be very important. You may have to spend a long time in the car travelling to a show and then spend all day at a muddy show ground; given the vagaries of the British weather you might have to be prepared for stifling hot sunshine one minute, and a sudden downpour the next; you must be comfortable in the ring and be able to run around to show off your dog. Some exhibitors also go as far as to choose an outfit that will highlight the colour of their dog's coat for maximum impact, and some have a 'lucky' outfit that they always wear when showing their dogs. Most seasoned exhibitors tend to go for practical and comfortable outfits that will last the whole day.

Don't forget all those other important bits and pieces you'll need during the course of the day. How about refreshments? Shows will have food and drinks for sale, but you may very well need to pack sandwiches and thermos flask if its going to be a long day, particularly if you're taking your whole family with you. Some people will take fold-up chairs or stools with them to watch the judging and if you don't fancy a day on your feet at the ringside, or have young children with you, this may be a good idea. If travelling by car, don't forget your road map, or you may spend the day driving around the countryside instead of going to a dog show!

Most important of all, do not forget to pack your schedule and ring number, and car park passes.

A practical yet smart outfit will take you through a whole day's showing and, with a bit of thought, show off your dog's lovely coat too.

Getting There

You will generally have to get up bright and early on show day if you are going to get yourself, your dog and all your equipment to the show on time. If you are having to travel any sort of distance, the chances are that you will have prepared your dog the day before the show and perhaps even have set out in the middle of the night. If this sounds like hard work, you may be surprised at just how many devoted dog show folk spend a huge amount of time and effort travelling around the country to attend dog shows.

Some coach companies lay on special trips to the larger dog shows for exhibitors, and some clubs will hire a minibus, or a coach, for their members to get to a show, but the vast majority of people go to shows under their own steam. Due to considerations of space most dog shows are held in rural or semi-rural sites. This generally means a car journey.

The schedule will tell you what time judging will start for your breed. Shows will generally be open a couple of hours before judging starts to allow everyone enough time to get into the show ground, get settled in and give their dogs a final brush. Judging at larger shows usually starts at 9.30 am so you will need to allow yourself plenty of time to find the show. Larger shows may well be signposted when you get near to the showground and the schedule may have a map printed inside to help you get to the venue.

Parking at smaller shows is usually on a first come, first served, basis, but at larger shows there may be stewards who direct you to the right place as there could be thousands of people attending. If you are going to a large show make sure you remember where you've parked, or you could be trailing round a vast car park at the end of the day, with your dog and all your show equipment, trying to spot your car.

Show organisers always ensure that refreshments are available – after all it's not just the dog's dinner you need to think about.

When you arrive at the show, remember your dog may be very keen to get out of the car to stretch his legs. It is important that you do not let your dog leap out of the car, as accidents can so easily happen.

Finding Your Way Around

Shows can initially be quite daunting as everyone but you seems to know where they're going and what they are doing.

The first thing you should do is get your bearings at the venue or showground. The most important areas to locate are the show secretary's or organiser's office, the benching area, the judging rings and the 'exercise areas' where you should take your dog if he needs to relieve himself. You should also keep an eye out for other facilities such as where you can get food and drinks from, where the loos are and any first aid posts.

At single breed or small shows it will all be pretty straightforward to find your way around as there will only be one or two rings, and any benching will be in straight numerical order. These sorts of shows may be held at venues like sports arenas, or village halls, so everything will be reasonably familiar.

Larger multi-breed shows, however, can be set up over quite a large area, sometimes at special showgrounds, or perhaps racecourses, and can take a little getting used to. The show will be housed in a number of large marquees and outside judging rings. Fortunately, these larger shows are usually well laid out and clearly sign-posted.

Catalogues

The catalogue can be a very useful aid to finding your way round the venue, as well as listing all the dogs which are

Make sure your dog travels in safety and comfort and that you keep him well under control at the venue.

Outdoor shows often use large marquees, as protection against the elements and for judging classes.

about to take part in the show. You should buy a catalogue as soon as you can to check your dog's class entry. If there has been some sort of error and his name appears under the wrong class, or doesn't appear at all, you should go straight to the show secretary's office to sort out the problem. If you have made an error and entered your dog in a class for which he is not eligible the show secretary will help you transfer your dog to another class. There are rules governing which class your dog can be transferred to, which the show secretary will explain to you, so do not expect to be always transferred to the class you originally wanted to enter.

Benching

If the show is benched, the benches will run in Group and then breed order and in numerical sequence for each breed. The bench number will always be the same as your ring number. If you become a bit lost just ask a steward, or another exhibitor, with the same breed of dog as you, where the breed is benched, or go to the organiser's offices and someone will point you in the right direction. The schedule and/or catalogue will tell you what ring your breed is being judged in, and although show organisers try to bench the dogs near to the ring where they are to be judged, it is well worth checking so that you avoid last minute panics. Fellow exhibitors are usually more than happy to help out people new to the show scene, so don't be shy about asking.

Grooming and Preparing your Dog for Exhibition

Once you have your dog settled on his bench and you have located your judging ring you can get your dog ready for exhibition. Short-coated breeds don't require too much preparation before they go into the ring but if your breed has a long coat, or is usually shown clipped in a certain style, it could take you some time to get your dog to perfection. Most grooming and clipping should be completed before you set out for the show, but some people give their dogs a quick brush and final trim just before going into the show ring. You should not obstruct the gangways between benches when you are preparing your dog for competition, for safety reasons. Instead, there will be clearly marked areas set aside for grooming tables. As a responsible dog exhibitor, you will, of course, collect up any loose fluff or hair generated in grooming and dispose of it in the appropriate place!

Ring Numbers

Once your dog is prepared it's a question of keeping your nerves at bay and waiting for the judging to begin.

The ring steward will announce when the judging is starting for each breed so you should listen hard for when your class is about to begin. Generally it is best to wait with your dog outside the ring while the class before yours is being judged. By doing this, you and your dog are ready for your class in plenty of time and don't run the risk of either, arriving at the last minute in a fluster, or, missing your class completely. If you do miss your class you cannot be transferred to another class.

If you are at a small show, the ring steward will ask you to

Ensure your ring number is prominently displayed whenever you're showing your dog.

identify yourself at the beginning of the class and give you your ring number. At larger shows, you will have been sent your ring number before the show. It is very important that you wear the correct ring number in a prominent position as the steward must ensure that the correctly numbered dogs go into the correct classes.

The steward will announce the start of each class, but do use a catalogue to keep an eye on the progress of judging so that you don't miss your class.

Each judge will have worked out their own system in the ring with their steward, so always listen to their directions.

Judges and Stewards

The judge is the person in control of everything that happens in the ring and exhibitors must do as he directs, but it is the steward's job to marshal all the exhibits coming into the ring, as he is the person responsible for carrying out the judge's directions in the ring. The judge will have told the steward how he will be judging and how he would like the waiting dogs to be organised.

The steward will call you into the ring to line up with the other exhibits in your class and then its simply a question of putting all that you learnt at your ringcraft classes into practice. The judge will examine your dog and look at your dog's conformation and movement When he has finished judging, you should rejoin the other dogs in your class at the end of the line. Always listen to what the judge tells you, as different judges have different preferences as to the style and order in which they wish to judge. Remember, you shouldn't try to engage the judge in conversation, simply answer any questions he asks of you.

Once the judge has gone over your dog, and all the other exhibits in the class and judged them against the Breed Standard, he will place the dogs in order of merit. He will call out the winning dogs into the centre of the ring and the other, unsuccessful dogs should leave the ring. There are at least 4 awards in every class and the judge will present the printed award cards and rosettes to the highest placed dog first. If you have been lucky enough to have won an award the steward will note down your ring number and details for the records.

The judge will call out the winning dogs in each class to the centre of the ring and line them up, in order of merit, from left to right, for the award cards and rosettes.

Awards and Competition Structure

Of course what everyone hopes for is to gain a prize in their class and preferably to walk away with first place. If you are lucky enough to gain a first place you then have the chance to go further in the competition on the day. But just what further awards might you win?

As has already been mentioned dog shows can be organised in a number of different ways, but in this book we are only going to be looking at the most common types of show, namely Single Breed Shows, and General Multi-Breed Shows judged on the Group System, and the awards you can gain at such shows.

The main principle of competition at these shows is that, if your dog is an unbeaten winning dog, it will be eligible to go forward to a higher level of competition at the show on the day, the Best in Show competition.

If your dog is entered for just one breed class and wins it, you will be called back, after the judging of all the other classes is complete, for the judge to pick the best of the assembled winners. If you have entered two classes, and your dog has only won one of them, he is considered a beaten dog and will not be called back to compete for Best of Breed.

If the breed has been split into Dogs and Bitches, all the winning dogs will be called back for the judge to choose Best Dog, and all the bitches will be called back to compete for Best Bitch. The judge will then decide between Best Dog and

Best Bitch to see which dog is Best of Breed. If Challenge Certificates are on offer for the breed the Best Dog and Best Bitch will be awarded Challenge Certificates.

At Single Breed Shows the Best of Breed is automatically Best in Show.

At larger, Multi-Breed Shows, all the Best of Breed winners, and the Best AVNSC (which is judged in the same way as the Best of Breed competition) go through to another round of competition. After all the breed judging for the day has finished, the Best of Breeds and Best AVNSC for each Group will all be gathered together in the main judging ring, usually with quite a crowd of spectators, and a new judge will measure each dog against their respective Breed Standards. The Best of Breed (or Best AVNSC) which the Group judge thinks most closely accords with its Breed Standard will be declared Best in Group.

At the end of the day, the seven Group winners will be seen by another judge who will choose which of them deserves the title of Best in Show.

As has been mentioned before, variety classes, do not fall within this competition structure. If you have entered a breed class and a variety class you cannot withdraw from the variety class because you hope to be chosen for Best of Breed as an unbeaten winning dog. You can withdraw from any Variety classes once you have become Best of Breed and are eligible to go through to the Best in Group and Best in Show competitions.

Good judges command their rings well – but don't be afraid to explain that you're new to the show scene if you don't know what to do.

The other main award at dog shows is that for Best Puppy in Show. This works on the same principle which governs the award for Best in Show, in that, all unbeaten winning puppies are eligible.

If you have entered one breed class with your puppy and have won it, you will be eligible to go through to Best Puppy in Breed. If your puppy has come second to an adult dog it will also be eligible to go through to best Puppy in Breed as it will still be classed as unbeaten winning puppy. The judge will gather all unbeaten winning puppies and choose Best Puppy in Group. The Best Puppy in Group winners will go through to the Best Puppy in Show competition in the same manner as adult dogs. At Championship Shows a Best Puppy in Breed will be chosen before going through to the Best Puppy in Group and Best Puppy in Show competitions.

It is only in the Best Puppy in Show competition that exhibits in the Variety classes are eligible. If there is no puppy class scheduled for your breed you may enter Any Variety Puppy and if successful you will be eligible to go forward to Best Puppy in Show.

The Best Puppy in Show competition is always judged after Best in Show, as if a puppy were to win Best in Show it would automatically be Best Puppy in Show as well.

You will be very lucky indeed if you scale such heights at shows, particularly as a newcomer to the show scene. However, as you start to get more experienced , and perhaps start to win prizes, you should keep good records about what your dog has won as you do not wish to enter a class which your dog has won too many prizes to be eligible for.

You should also keep records if you want to try to win a Kennel Club Junior Warrant. This is a Kennel Club award issued to dogs that have obtained 25 points whilst between the ages of 6 and 18 months. The scale of points is as follows:

Why not take the time to watch the judging of other classes – you might pick up some showing tips and you can see whether you select the same winners as the judge.

- Three points for each first prize awarded in a Breed Class at a Championship Show where Challenge Certificates are on offer for the breed.
- One point for each First Prize awarded in a Breed Class at a Championship Show where Challenge Certificates were not on offer for the breed, or at an Open Show.
- A minimum of 12 points must be won at Championship Shows where Challenge Certificates are on offer.

If your dog gains 25 points you must complete an application form and send it to The Kennel Club and you will receive a Certificate to show how well your dog has done and you will have qualified your dog to take part in Crufts.

Looking Around

As a beginner, your class is likely to be relatively early on in the day, however, you should take the opportunity of watching the day's judging. One of the delights of dog showing is watching the judging and most exhibitors take a keen interest in what the judge is doing. Following the judging, will give you the chance to run a critical eye over the opposition and to find out what the judge is looking for. Watching seasoned exhibitors will also give you a much greater insight into how to handle your dog more professionally, how to behave in the ring and to become familiar with the actual mechanics of showing your dog.

At larger Multi-Breed Shows you also have the chance to see all sorts of other breeds in action in the show ring and strolling around the showground provides a good opportunity to talk to other dog owners and learn about other breeds of dog.

You should also take the chance at Multi-Breed Shows to see the Group and Best in Show competitions. These competitions are the highlight to any show and even if your dog has not made it through you can still go to cheer on your breed and see the best of all the dogs at the show.

At larger shows there are also likely to be plenty of trade stands selling all manner of 'doggy' paraphernalia, from dog food to coats, leads, grooming equipment, and kennels. There may also be gardening stalls, book stalls, stands selling clothing and all sorts of arts and crafts for sale. So once you have watched your breed being judged there's plenty of opportunity to catch up on the shopping!

Leaving the Show

Most smaller shows allow you to leave as soon as you want to, but some larger shows stipulate that dogs should not leave the showground before a certain time. Always check the schedule carefully for this sort of information, as leaving a show without permission may result in your being reported to The Kennel Club.

Most larger shows will also ask you to show your number, or some other form of identification, before you leave the venue with a dog, for security reasons.

Shows aren't just about competition and prizes. Whether you're looking for basics like dog food, a treat for yourself, or you just want to browse, there will be plenty of trade stands to look at and lots of fascinating people to meet.

Obedience Competitions

What is Obedience?
Undertaking a training course, like the Good Citizen Dog Scheme, helps you build up a good rapport with your dog and, as you are both going through your paces during classes, you may really enjoy the feeling of achievement you get from acting as a team. Most clubs do much more than basic training, and it is probably through watching other club members and their dogs working together, perhaps at Obedience Matches, that you will want to get involved in canine obedience at a higher level.

Obedience is an absorbing and involving sport, and many hundreds of competitors all over the country have been hooked by this interesting hobby. Obedience competitions examine how well you and your dog work together as a team, by putting you through various set exercises. A judge will deduct points each time you make a mistake. In all shows (or tests as they are more commonly known), the dog should work in a happy and natural manner and the lowest classes are usually relaxed and informal events. The Kennel Club has set rules about how each exercise within each class should be conducted, so although the exercises may look straightforward at first glance, you and your dog are actually expected to work to a high standard. However, a few minutes training your dog every day, with plenty of praise and encouragement, will see your dog develop into a real professional!

Above all, Obedience Tests are considered to be 'fun competitions', designed to be enjoyed by dog and owner. Informality is encouraged, however nothing may be included in an Obedience Test which could endanger the safety of the dogs competing, the handlers, or the spectators.

Classes
Before you think about entering an obedience competition you must know what will be asked of you and your dog, and have trained and be ready to meet the challenge the exercises will set you.

Unlike other forms of canine competition, in Obedience you must enter the lowest one of six classes your dog is eligible for, and by a series of first prizes qualify to higher classes. Having entered the lowest class you can also enter the next highest class if you wish to (except for Championship Class C which you must qualify into). Many competitors do this to give their dogs as much experience as possible and because they enjoy the thrill of competition.

Pre-Beginners Class
As a newcomer to Obedience you will start off in Pre-Beginners class which can be scheduled at various levels of Obedience Shows. To take part the handler and dog must not have won a First Prize in Pre-Beginners before, nor gained a third place, or above, in any other Obedience class. Sometimes it is queried whether a dog which has not won a first prize before can be handled by a more experienced handler, with wins under their belt. This is not the case and

Stuck on you! Your dog should keep as close to you as possible during heelwork exercises.

this class is only for the least experienced in the Obedience world.

There are 5 exercises in this class with a total of 75 points available.

Heel on lead.

This exercise tests how well your dog walks to heel on a lead.

At the beginning of the exercise, your dog should be sitting straight at your left hand side which in obedience competitions is considered your 'working side'. On the judge's command, you should walk briskly forward in a straight line with your dog at heel. The dog's shoulder should be approximately level and reasonably close to your leg at all times when you are walking. The lead should be slack at all times and you will be penalised if you have to check your dog with the lead during the exercise. During the test, the judge will ask you to do a number of manoeuvres, either to turn 90 degrees to your left or your right, or to do a 180 degree about turn. Your dog should keep his position by your side at all times. At the end of the test the judge will tell you to 'Halt', and your dog should sit straight at your side. The judge can deduct up to 15 points from your score depending on how many mistakes you make during this exercise.

Heel free

This exercise will be in the same format as the previous exercise, but with the obvious factor that your dog will not be on the lead throughout the test. This is a real test of how well trained your dog is and the judge may deduct up to 20 points for mistakes.

Show a clean pair of heels to the judge!

You will have to put in a lot of dedicated training to succeed at the highest levels.

Recall

This exercise tests your dog's obedience in following your commands to remain in one position and then to come to you when called. You can choose whether to put your dog in a down or sitting position. At the judge, or steward's, command you should walk a set distance away from your dog, turn to face your dog and call him to you. Your dog should not have moved while you walked away from him. As soon as you call him, your dog should come straight to you, sit in front of you and then go to heel as soon as the judge, or steward, tells you. This exercise carries up to 10 penalty points.

The following two exercises test how well your dog will follow your command to stay in one position and then to come to you when called. Unlike the other exercises you cannot use additional commands, or encouragement, in these exercises. The sit and down stays are held at the same time for all the dogs taking part in the test, so you will be gathered together with all the other competitors and their dogs from your class, in one ring, for these exercises.

Sit/Stay

The judge, or steward, will direct you to a specific point in the ring and then say 'Last Command'. This means that you must give your final command to your dog to sit and stay where he is. You will then be directed to walk to another point in the ring. You will be timed for one minute, and when this has elapsed you should walk back to your dog, who should not have moved during the exercise. Up to 10 points can be lost here.

Down/Stay

This exercise is in the same format to the previous one but your dog must remain in a down position throughout the test and be expected to remain stationary for 2 minutes. Up to a further 20 points could be lost for mistakes.

After each one of these exercises is complete you should

praise your dog and reward him for following your commands so well.

As with all Obedience Tests you will have to work in a set manner for each exercise. Your dog may only wear a slip chain, or smooth collar, in the ring and you must not carry any food, or treats, for your dog into the ring. You can encourage and praise your dog as much as you like for all the exercises except the Sit and Down/Stay tests.

Beginners Class

Once you have succeeded in the Pre-Beginners class you will be able to progress to the Beginners Class. To enter this class, handler and dog must not have won a total of two, or more, First Prizes in Beginners, or, one First Prize in any other Obedience class (Pre-Beginners excepted). The Beginners class combines all the exercises used in the Pre-Beginners class but has an additional element, worth an extra 25 points, of retrieving an article.

At the start of this additional exercise your dog should be sitting by your side. The judge will ask you to throw an article in a particular direction, and your dog should remain by your side until the caller steward, or judge, gives the order for you to send your dog to retrieve the article. Your dog should go straight to the article and bring it back to you, sitting directly in front of you to present the retrieved article. You may only take the article from your dog on the judge's command and your dog should then go to heel.

Other Classes

As you become more experienced you will be able to progress from the Beginners classes to Novice, Class A, Class B and Open and Championship Class C. These classes get progressively more difficult, introducing more complicated and exacting exercises and expecting an exemplary level of performance.

Some of the exercises that are introduced as you progress through the classes are: scent discrimination, where your

Carry the day as well as the dumb-bell with a good clean retrieve.

Will you and your dog stay the distance?

Hide bound! At higher levels of competition your dog will have to remain in a stay whilst you keep out of sight for a set period.

dog is expected to retrieve a particular article from a selection laid out in the ring; distance control, when your dog must obey commands to sit, stand, or down, given while you are standing some distance away from him; heel work at different speeds and with many different manoeuvres.

What's on, Where and When?

Obedience is not as big a sport as dog showing but there are still plenty of competitions held round the country and a large and keen group of enthusiasts. Like most dog shows, Obedience competitions happen all year round but tend to be concentrated in the summer to take advantage of any good weather, and are usually held at weekends to allow as many people as possible to enter. It is mainly training clubs that organise Obedience competitions but, some breed clubs and general canine societies may also schedule an obedience show alongside a larger dog show.

Your dog does not need to be a pedigree, or pure-bred dog, to take part in Obedience competitions, and indeed many cross-breeds have become very successful in the Obedience ring. You must, however, ensure that your dog is registered with The Kennel Club on the Breed Register, or the Obedience and Working Trials Register, if it is to be eligible for competition.

There are several ways of finding our what Obedience competitions are being held. The Kennel Gazette lists details of forthcoming events in the Show Guide section of the magazine; the general dog press , 'Dog World' and 'Our Dogs', will also carry adverts for forthcoming shows; and the specialist Obedience magazine, 'Dog Training Weekly' will have full listings.

You will most likely find out about Obedience competitions through your local training club, which gives you the opportunity to ask the advice of more seasoned competitors whether you and your dog are ready for competition.

Types of Test

There are 3 different types of Obedience test where the competition becomes successively more difficult. There will be all sorts of classes at these tests, from the most junior Pre-Beginners class, to the most senior Class C.

Limited Obedience Test

Limited tests can restrict entry in a number of ways. They may be limited to only the members of the organising society; they may be limited to residents within a specific area; they may be limited by the number of entrants; or they may be limited to specific breeds of dog. No dogs which have won, The Kennel Club's top award, an Obedience Certificate, may take part, so less experienced dogs and owners have more of a chance of going home with prizes.

Open Obedience Test

As the name suggests these competitions are open to anyone who wishes to enter them. As there are no restrictions these shows attract many competitors of every level and experience.

Championship Obedience Test

These tests are also open to anyone to enter but will also have on offer, The Kennel Club's top Obedience award - Obedience Certificates (also known as tickets). These awards can only be won by dogs winning the highest class, Championship Class C.

How to Enter an Obedience Show

In common with other Kennel Club licensed events, societies must issue a schedule in advance of Obedience competitions. The schedule provides all the information you will need to enter the test - when and where its being held, the judges' names, what classes are scheduled and what date completed entry forms must be received by the show organisers, which is referred to as the 'Closing Date'.

Schedules for Obedience competitions are quite straight forward. The front cover will have the name of the society holding the competition, what sort of test it is, the name and address of the organisers, and the closing date for entries. The inside of the schedule will list the Kennel Club rules and regulations governing the test. a list of the classes being scheduled and the qualifications for each one.

If your club has not been given copies of schedules for a show you want to enter you simply phone the society secretary and ask to be sent a copy of the schedule and an entry form. You may be asked to provide a stamped addressed envelope to help keep the club's expenses down.

When you receive your entry form you must complete it legibly and accurately. You will be asked to provide the breed of your dog and his registered name, that of his sire and dam, and his date of birth. If your dog is a cross-breed on The Kennel Club Working Trials and Obedience Register you should provide exactly the same information that appears on the Register, marking dam and sire as 'Unknown' if that is the case. If you do make a mistake in the completion of this information you may lose any awards that your dog might gain at the competition, so it is vital that you take the time to get the details correct.

You should complete other details, such as your name and address and which class you wish to enter, clearly and legibly to avoid any problems and make sure you have enclosed the correct fee. Incorrect fees are the problem most commonly encountered by organisers when dealing with entries.

It is also vital that you sign the entry form as it forms the contract between you and the organising society. If the dog is jointly owned, both parties should sign the entry form unless one of the parties has the express permission of the other to sign on their behalf. By signing, you are declaring that your dog is fit and healthy to take part in competition and that you will abide by Kennel Club rules and regulations. This is essential to the management of the test and for the sport in general.

You should post your entry form off in plenty of time of the closing date for entries. It is also recommended that you should consider getting a Certificate of Posting, from the Post Office. It can be terribly disappointing to travel all the way to

If you reward your dog with plenty of praise, he'll want to work all the harder for you.

*Watching
Obedience
can be thirsty
work!*

a show to find that the show secretary never received your entry form. If, however, you take the time to obtain a Certificate of Posting, available free of charge from the Post Office, the competition organisers will be able to accept your entry on the day of the test, although The Kennel Club will still have to look over everything after the show to check that all was in order. When completing a 'Proof of Posting' slip at the Post Office make sure that you clearly write the name of the society and the words 'entry form'. The number of items being sent should be written in words and not numerals if it is to be considered valid. This may all seem a bit complicated for just sending off an entry form, but, after all, it's better to be safe than sorry!

The schedule may also ask that you send a stamped addressed envelope with your entry form so that the show manager can send you your ring number and any other passes needed at the show.

When the test organiser receives all the entries, a ballot will be conducted to decide the first 10 runners in each class. This is done to ensure that the judging gets underway promptly on the day of the test. If your name has been picked in the ballot the organisers will notify you before the test so that you know to be there in plenty of time.

Your Day at an Obedience Test

Preparation

If you are going to spend the day at an Obedience test you must think about all the things you will need during the course of the day.

Firstly, your dog will need his collar and lead, and, if you train using a particular toy as encouragement, that should not be forgotten either. Trainers at your club may advise you not to feed your dog before going to an Obedience competition as it may make him sleepy and not want to give his best in competition. However, if you are going to feed your dog remember to pack his food and water bowls. Don't forget though that you are not permitted to bring any tit-bits of food into the judging ring!

Although Obedience tests are not beauty competitions your dog should be well prepared for the show, groomed, clean and generally in excellent condition.

You will also need to think about your own needs at the test; your choice of clothing and footwear is important as you will need to be comfortable and have a firm footing to work in the ring with your dog, as well as withstanding the vagaries of the British weather. Most Obedience tests are held in the open air, so be prepared! Although there will be refreshments available at the showground you might want to pack food and beverages for the day; and road maps to ensure that you're able to find the show ground.

Getting There

A lot of schedules carry maps explaining how to get to the showground, or venue, and obedience competitions held as part of larger dog shows are usually signposted when you get near to the showground.

The time judging starts will be in the schedule but you will have to set off in plenty of time if you are to get to your classes on time. Competitions always open at least a couple of hours before judging starts to allow competitors plenty of time to arrive and get their dogs settled before competition.

Finding Your Way Around

Specialist Obedience shows can attract large entries with many hundreds of dogs. There will be a judging ring for each class as well as a ring for the Stay exercises, so you may be faced with as many as 20 rings at a venue.

Obedience tests, held as part of a larger dog show, may be at large showgrounds with many marquees and judging rings and room for hundreds of cars to park. These shows can be quite bewildering for newcomers but there are usually plenty of stewards and other officials, both at the entrance to the showground, and in the showground itself, to guide you in the right direction. If you are in any doubt as to where to go you should find the show organiser's offices and somebody there will be able to help you.

Whatever venue the test is being held at you should familiarise yourself with the showground. Take a good look at the layout of the judging rings , locate the Stays ring and the 'Exercise Areas' where you should take your dog to relieve himself; look out for the show manager's office, refreshment areas, loos and first aid posts.

The catalogue is often a useful guide to help you find your way around the showground and lists the names and other details of all the other dogs and people who are going to take part in the obedience competition that day.

Booking in and Running Orders

After having familiarised yourself with the layout of the show the next thing that you should do is to 'book in'. You should find the organisers' office where the scoreboard steward will check your ring number and mark you as present in the catalogue. The ring number is the number by which you and your dog will be identified during the day as

It may be a 'doggone' shame if it's raining, but it won't stop the competition from carrying on!

You should 'book-in' at the organisers' office as soon as possible.

the judge can only refer to you by your ring number as he is not permitted to know the names of the people, or dogs, he is about to judge. It is, therefore, very important that you wear your ring number, prominently displayed, at all times during competition.

The scoreboard steward will encourage you to put your name down in the running order for your class. The first ten places will have been decided before the show by ballot, but the order of the rest of the runners is decided on the day. It is very helpful to get your names down in the running order so that the class proceeds smoothly and that there are no long gaps in between competitors.

Once you have booked in you should go to the ring where your class is being judged. It is very important that you come to the ring to be judged at the right time as lateness could result in elimination.

If there are over 60 dogs entered in one class, it will be split between 2 judges. Make sure you know in which group you are to be judged.

Warming Up

Most people like to work with their dog when they actually arrive at the show ground to get their dogs 'warmed-up' for competition and to concentrate their minds on the task in hand. Remember though that you should not disturb other people when you are working with your dog as they are trying to concentrate too.

Judges and Stewards

Every class will have a judge, a caller steward and a score steward. The judge is in control of the ring and he will have checked that the ring is the right size and worked out how he will direct people during the class exercises. The caller steward announces when a class is about to start and marshals waiting competitors, will issue commands during the Heelwork exercises and commands during other exercises, at the judge's direction. It will be made clear by the judge at the beginning of each exercise who will be issuing directions and directions will be given at the same time, and the same place, for each competitor.

The scribe steward will make a note of all the points that the judge indicates have been lost to a particular competitor

All clubs need plenty of help, so if you would like to try stewarding, show organisers would be delighted to hear from you.

so that the judge does not need to take his eyes off the dog. The score steward will then keep a note of the total points each competitor in the class gains and work out final placings.

For the Stay exercises the whole class will be judged in a separate ring. The chief steward will have organised a team of Stay stewards who will time the exercise and monitor each dog for movement. The judge will also be present to oversee proceedings.

Awards and Competition

The competition structure for Obedience competitions is much more straightforward than that for dog showing. Each class starts with a certain number of points for each competitor, and points are deducted as dogs and handlers make mistakes. The first prize in each class simply goes to the competitor who loses the least points. In the event of a tie, the judge will organise a run-off between the two tied competitors. If it is a tie for first place the judge may ask the competitors to go through all the exercises again in that class; if its a tie for third or fourth place the judge may only ask the competitors to do one or two more exercises.

There are at least four awards in every class and as well as printed award cards and rosettes, there may also be prize money and sometimes trophies, on offer.

It is important as you go to Obedience tests that you keep a record of how well you and your dog do, as each first place counts towards you becoming eligible for a higher class. You will also need to keep a record of your wins if you are to apply for the Kennel Club award of an Obedience Warrant. This award can be applied for if a dog has gained 14 points whilst ineligible to compete for Championship Class C. The points are gained as follows:

- Two points for a first Prize in Novice Class on two occasions only.
- Two points for a first Prize in Class A on two occasions only.
- Two points for a first Prize in Class B on two occasions only.
- Two points for a first Prize in Open Class C on one occasion only.

After Competition

Going to an Obedience competition is a great opportunity to look at real experts working with, and training, their dogs. You should take the time to talk to judges and experienced trainers and handlers who may be able to give you valuable advice. By looking at what's happening during judging you will be able to see just what standard you and your dog must aspire to for each class and perhaps pick up some tips on how to achieve that.

Many events will also have plenty of trade stands selling everything from dog food, bedding and toys to stands selling clothing, and arts and crafts. Competitions will also have refreshments available. With so much to see and do you can make an Obedience test a real family day out.

After competing why not get to know your fellow competitors...

...you might even pick up one or two valuable pointers for the next test.

Agility

What is an Agility Test?

You may have seen Agility demonstrations on the television, at Crufts, or Discover Dogs, and wondered if you and your dog could take part in the exciting sport, where dogs and owners run around an obstacle course against the clock. Well the good news is that you can. Hundreds of clubs up and down the country can help you with Agility training, and there are hundreds of competitions for you to enter.

The sport of Agility was first introduced to the UK in 1978 at Crufts, and many people think that Agility is the most fun, for both humans and dogs, of all the canine sports. It's fast, furious and a great favourite with competitors and spectators alike, at all sorts of dog shows. Your dog does not have to be a pedigree, or pure-bred dog, but it must be registered with The Kennel Club on the Breed Register, or the Obedience and Working Trials Register, to join in.

Size doesn't matter either, because there are Agility tests for Standard Dogs, measuring 1ft 5ins at the withers, the highest point of the shoulder; Midi Dogs, measuring over 1ft 3ins, but under 1ft 5ins at the withers; and Mini Dogs, measuring under 1ft 3ins at the withers.

One important stipulation, however, is that dogs must be over 18 months of age and fit to take part, as it is such a physical sport and so much training is necessary before a dog can compete.

Fast and furious and above all, fun – is Agility the sport for you?

The Course

An Agility test will have a series of obstacles laid out in a large area called a ring. The Kennel Club allows a combination of 16 obstacles to be used on an Agility course. All the measurements given for the following obstacles are for Standard Dogs. The obstacles for Midi and Mini Dogs are, naturally, smaller.

Hurdles

These are a maximum of 2ft 6ins in height and 4ft in width and competing dogs must leap over the hurdles without knocking them over. The top part of the hurdle must always be easily displaced so that your dog does not hurt himself if he does knock down the bar.

Rising spread jump

This is a series of 2 hurdles positioned closely together, with the first hurdle set lower than the second.

Brush fence

This is another sort of hurdle, again with an easily displaced top unit.

Hoop (Tyre)

Your dog must jump through the hoop or tyre suspended from a frame at a fixed height.

Table

The table is a minimum of 3ft square and must be of stable construction with a non-slip surface. Your dog must lie down on the table for a time set by the judge.

Long jump

The dog must jump a maximum length of five ft, clearing a series of low hurdles.

Water jump

A low hurdle may be placed in front of a long jump of shallow water.

Jumping for joy!

Does your dog have tunnel vision?

Are you and your dog for the long jump?

The collapsible tunnel
is no obstacle here.

Wishing Well or Lych Gate
This hurdle must have a roof to it, and again a displaceable top bar should be used.

Collapsible Tunnel
This has a rigid round entrance with non-slip cloth forming the body of the tunnel which can be up to 10 ft long. Your dog must make his way through the tunnel.

Pipe Tunnel
A minimum of 2ft wide and up to 10ft long.

Weaving poles
A series of between 5 and 12 poles set at least 1ft 6ins apart that your dog has to weave in and out of.

Pause Box
An area 4ft by 4ft on the ground of the ring where your dog has to pause for a period specified by the judge.

Up, up...
...and over!

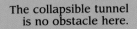

'A' Frame

An 'A' shaped frame formed by 2 ramps with non-slip surfaces and anti-slip slats, that dogs must climb over. There are 'contact points' at the base of each ramp, coloured differently to the rest of the obstacle, that the dogs' paws must come into contact with if penalty points are not to be incurred.

See-Saw

A pivoted plank, minimum length of 12ft, which your dog must negotiate. Again your dog must touch the coloured 'contact points'.

Dog Walk

A plank approximately 4ft 6ins high, with firmly fixed ramps at either end which dogs must walk over, ensuring that paws touch 'contact points'.

Pole to pole – let's get weaving!

Cross Over

This obstacle resembles a raised, square table with ramps leading up to all 4 sides. Your dog must go up and down the particular ramps indicated by the judge. Again contact points will be marked on the obstacle that the dogs' paws must touch.

First Steps

You should never attempt an Agility course unless you have had proper training. This is a physical and demanding sport and both you, and your dog, need to be healthy and agile to take part. With so many complicated pieces of equipment used in an Agility test, you and your dog will have to train hard to ensure that, not only do you reach the necessary standard to be successful, but that you do so safely. The Kennel Club has set rules about how the obstacles should be safely laid out and what their sizes should be, and the judge must always keep a keen watch on all aspects of safety, but you too must put your dog's welfare first and make sure you compete sensibly and safely.

Take walking the dog to the next level on the see-saw and dog walk.

Many clubs are set up specifically to cater for Agility enthusiasts. As well as providing all the support and training that other clubs do, specialist Agility clubs will have their own sets of Agility obstacles which can be used in training, and also at various levels of competition.

Having attended training sessions your first taste of competition will probably be at a club Agility Match. These are friendly knockout competitions held for the membership of a particular club, or between the members of a number of clubs. From there you may wish to enter a fully fledged competition.

There are all sorts of ways you can find out about Agility competitions. The Show Guide Section of the Kennel Gazette provides listings of all forthcoming events; weekly newspapers, 'Dog World' and 'Our Dogs' carry advertisements of shows; there are also 2 specialist Agility publications, 'Agility Voice' and 'Agility Eye' which carry full details as well as all the news and views from the world of Agility.

Types of Agility Test

There are only 3 types of Agility test. Agility Matches are restricted to members of the show society only. Entry to Limited Agility Tests is restricted to members of the show society, or competitors from a certain area, or, limited to certain breeds, or, sizes of dog. Open Agility Tests, are just that, open to all who wish to take part.

As has already been mentioned, there are 3 different size categories for competing dogs and clubs may schedule classes for one, some, or all of these sizes.

Classes

There are many different classes which can be scheduled at Agility tests. There are Agility classes defined by The Kennel Club which become progressively more competitive as you become more successful and win out of each class; there are Jumping classes which are fairly self-explanatory and do not require the dogs to undertake the sea-saw, dog walk or A frame obstacles; there are special classes which are defined by the show management in the schedule. In such special classes, either the definition for eligibility to compete is not per Kennel Club Regulations, the marking of the class differs from standard Kennel Club marking or the course design is non-standard. Classes such as these, with unusual names like Helter Skelter, Triathlon, Gamblers, Knock-Out and Pairs, will be clearly defined in the schedule so you know exactly what to expect when you enter.

Whatever classes you decide to go for, they will be at the following levels:

A good clear round in Agility is always a crowd-pleaser and plenty of encouragement is shouted from the ringside.

Elementary

This is the lowest Agility class and is designed for owners, handlers or dogs, which have not gained a third prize, or above, in an Agility and/or Jumping class at a licensed Agility test.

Starters

For owners, handlers or dogs, which have not won an Agility and/or Jumping Class at a licensed Agility Test (Elementary excepted).

Novice

Open to dogs which are not eligible for Senior or Advanced classes.

Intermediate

Open to all except dogs eligible for Elementary and Starters at a licensed Agility Test.

Seniors

Open to all dogs having won at least two first prizes at a licensed Agility Test (Elementary and Starter wins excepted)

Advanced

Open to dogs having a minimum of four wins at a licensed Agility Test, two of which must be gained in Intermediate, Senior or Open Agility (not Jumping) Classes (Elementary, Starter and Novice wins excepted).

Open

Open to all.

Entering a Test

Once you have found a suitable Agility Test you would like to compete in, you should get hold of a copy of the show schedule. All Agility clubs must issue a show schedule prior to a test with all the details of the competition. Schedules are often circulated to local training clubs, but, if you haven't seen one, you simply phone the club secretary and ask for one to be sent to you. You may be asked to send a stamped addressed envelope, to keep the club's costs down.

The schedule for Agility Tests is very straightforward and easy to understand. The front cover will show the name of the society holding the test, the names and addresses of the organisers, what sort of competition it is, the show date, the venue, and the closing date for entries. All the scheduled classes will be listed and Kennel Club Agility rules and regulations will be printed inside.

Your entry form must be completed legibly and accurately, to avoid any possible misunderstanding. You will be asked to provide the breed of your dog, his Kennel Club registered name, Kennel Club registration number and his date of birth. If your dog is on the Breed Register, or a cross-breed on The Kennel Club Working Trials and Obedience Register you should provide exactly the same information that appears on the Register, marking your dog's dam and sire as 'Unknown' if that is the case. If you do make a mistake in the completion

Age is no obstacle in Agility. As long as you and your dog are reasonably fit you can face the challenge of the course.

of this information you may lose any awards that your dog might gain at the competition, so it is vital that you take the time to get the details correct.

You should complete other details, such as your name and address and which class you wish to enter, clearly and legibly to avoid any problems and make sure you have enclosed the correct fee. It is worth, checking, and double checking, that you have put down the correct class name and number on the entry form as it is not easy to rectify mistakes. You should also ensure that you send the correct fee. The problem most frequently faced by test organisers when dealing with entry forms is incorrect fees.

It is also vital that you sign the entry form as it forms the contract between you and the society. If the dog is jointly owned, both parties should sign the entry form unless one of the parties has the express permission of the other to sign on their behalf. By signing, you are declaring that your dog is fit and healthy to take part in competition and that you will abide by Kennel Club rules and regulations. This is essential to the management of the show and for the sport in general.

You should post your entry form off within plenty of time of the closing date for entries. It is also recommended that you should consider getting a Certificate of Posting, from the Post Office. It can be terribly disappointing to travel all the way to a test to find that the secretary never received your entry form. If, however, you take the time to obtain a Certificate of Posting, available free of charge from the Post Office, the organisers will be able to accept your entry on the day of the test, although The Kennel Club will still have to look over everything after the test to check that all was in order. When completing a 'Proof of Posting' slip at the Post Office make sure that you clearly write the name of the society and the words 'entry form'. The number of items being sent should be written in words and not numerals if it is to be considered valid. This may all seem a bit complicated for just sending off an entry form, but, after all, it's better to be safe than sorry!

A good clear round needs non-slip footwear, whether competing inside or out.

Some societies will also ask that you send a stamped addressed envelope so that they can send you all the passes and other information you will need prior to the show. If this is asked for on the schedule, please do remember to include it as this will prevent problems for both you and the organisers.

Your Day at an Agility Test

Planning

There are a lot of things to plan before you actually set out for a day at an Agility test.

Think about all that your dog will need during the journey to and from the competition and at the venue - collar, lead, food, bowls. Does he have a favourite toy you like to train with?

You should also consider what you are going to wear. Your outfit must be comfortable to travel to the test, and be flexible enough to withstand the vagaries of the British weather. Sensible footwear is a must for running round Agility courses, and remember if the grass is wet you are going to need shoes with a good grip.

Don't forget all the other bits and pieces you need for a day out. Refreshments will be available for sale at the showground but you might want to think about packing sandwiches and drinks, particularly if you are taking the whole family. Some people even pack folding chairs to watch the competition in case seats aren't provided by the organisers. It can also be important to pack road maps and a copy of the schedule or you may lose your way to the showground. Above all don't forget your passes and ring numbers if they have been sent by post before the test.

A lot of show schedules carry maps explaining how to get to the showground, or venue, and agility competitions held as part of larger dog shows are usually signposted when you get near to the showground.

You will need to allow plenty of time for travelling to the showground. The time judging starts will be printed in the schedule but the showground will be open several hours beforehand, and you should try to get to the show with plenty of time in hand so that you are calm and collected for competition.

Finding Your Way Around

Agility tests can attract many hundreds of dogs and there may be many rings laid out with different obstacle courses for each class. As the competition rings are quite large, Agility tests tend to be held on sports fields, or at rural showgrounds.

Sometimes breed clubs, or general canine societies, may schedule Agility tests as well as training clubs. Such events can be held at very large show grounds with many marquees and trade stands. This can all be quite bewildering to newcomers to the dog show scene but there are usually plenty of stewards and other show officials to point you in the right direction.

Whatever venue the show is being held at you should

Refreshments will be provided at the showground, but pack your own chairs if you don't fancy standing at the ringside, or sitting on the grass all day.

familiarise yourself with the layout of the judging rings, find out where you should take your dog to relieve himself (referred to as 'exercise areas') and look out for the organiser's office, refreshment areas, loos and first aid posts.

Booking In

After having familiarised yourself with the layout of the show the next thing that you should do is to 'book in'. If you have not received a ring number and other information by post prior to the test, you should go to the organiser's office and you will be given a ring number. This is the number by which you and your dog will be identified at the show as the judge is not allowed to know who he is about to judge. It is therefore important that your ring number is prominently displayed at all times.

Some special competitions, such as Knockouts, also require competitors to formally register that they have arrived on the day. If this is the case and even if you have already received your ring number, you must book in as requested.

Running Order

The show management will have drawn a running order for competitors to ensure that the classes are run in an orderly fashion and that competitors have a good indication when they can expect to start their round. The running order will be displayed in the rings and may also be on the reverse of your ring number card. You should make sure that you get to the judging ring in plenty of time as lateness may result in elimination.

If you are entered in more than one class and you think that your running orders will clash you should speak to the ring steward and usually something can be worked out.

As well as the usual competition classes, there may also be novelty classes scheduled, such as Pairs or ABC (Anything but a Collie!).

Warming Up

As Agility requires such a close partnership between handler and dog, many people like to run through their paces prior to competition to warm their dogs up. If you do this make sure that you do not interrupt other competitors who may also be trying to concentrate on their teamwork and general obedience.

Each Agility course will be laid out differently and it is vital that you attend any briefings the Judge gives about how the course is laid out and which way he expects dogs to move round the course. If you need any points clarifying you should ask - the judge will always be happy to answer questions. It should also be possible to walk the course prior to competition to familiarise yourself with the course layout. You may spot potential short cuts and this may well save you valuable seconds in competition. You should also look out for places on the course where you will need to change your position in relation to your dog's, to be able to direct him over obstacles more quickly, or where you can send your dog on ahead.

Judges and Stewards

The judge is in overall control of the ring and you must follow any instructions he has given you at the briefing. The judge will be looking to see that you go through the obstacle course in the right order, that all contact points are met and that your dog stays on the Table, or in the Box, for the correct length of time.

The judge will be assisted by a number of stewards all fulfilling different roles.

The timekeeper will have a stopwatch to accurately measure who gains the fastest time round the course. He stays in the ring throughout the class, ensuring that he

Before competition the judge will explain the layout of the obstacles and you should make the time to walk the course as this will help you shave vital seconds from your lap time.

Running commentary provided...

"Congratulations!"

remains in the same position for the start and end of every competitor's run, to ensure timings are accurate.

The scribe steward watches the judge throughout every round and records every time the judge indicates that a dog has gained a fault.

The caller steward ensures that the running order is kept to as well as marshalling the next competitors so that the judge is not kept waiting in between rounds. There may well be a Collecting Ring next to the Judging Ring where the caller steward will assemble all the dogs for the next class, so keep an ear open for instructions.

A scoreboard steward will keep a record of all the scores for each round and calculate final placings. They may be helped by runners who collect judging slips from the scribe steward and bring them back to the central scoreboard area.

Jump stewards ensure that any hurdles are replaced if they are knocked over, the tunnel is straightened and generally supervise the obstacles on the course. The obstacles will usually be straightened at the end of rounds so as not to impede any competitors.

Remember most clubs are always on the look out for people to help in the organising of shows, so if you want to try stewarding just let the event organiser know.

Scoring

There are Kennel Club guidelines on what comprises a fault and how many faults the judge should deduct from the competitor, and these will be printed in the Schedule.

The judge will set a time by which he expects exhibitors to complete the course. Faults are incurred for failure to negotiate obstacles correctly and failure to complete the course within the set time. The judge will make the marking system clear at his briefings prior to competition.

There are various faults which result with elimination from competition:

- Three refusals of an obstacle
- Taking the wrong route round the course
- Your dog fouling the ring
- Your dog becoming out of control

After Competition

Going to an Agility test is a great opportunity to look at real experts working with, and training, their dogs. Talking to and socialising with fellow competitors judges and stewards will provide valuable information and ideas to improve your performance. By looking at what's happening during judging you will be able to see just what standard you and your dog must aspire to for each class and perhaps pick up some tips on how to achieve that.

Take the time to have a good look round the showground. Many shows will have plenty of trade stands selling everything from dog food, bedding and toys to stands selling clothing, and arts and crafts. Shows will also have refreshments available. With so much to see and do you can make an Agility Test a really enjoyable day out for you and your family.

It's not just your dog who"ll have a great day out at an Agility Test – there's fun for the whole family to enjoy!

Flyball Competitions

What is Flyball?

Flyball is another energetic and fun activity you can enjoy, both as a spectator, and by joining in with your dog.

Flyball was introduced to this country in 1990 at Crufts. It is essentially a spectator sport involving a team knockout competition and many people who have a background in Agility have become involved in competitions and display teams.

Flyball involves several teams running against each other, and the clock, in relay. Each dog on the team has to leap over a series of hurdles to the 'flyball box'. The dog presses a pedal on the box and a tennis ball is flung into the air. The dog must catch the ball and race back over the hurdles to the start/finish line and the next team member released, until the entire team has completed the course. The dogs seem to love this sport and competitions are usually accompanied by plenty of happy and excited barking.

This is very much a fun event and competitors and organisers are encouraged to treat Flyball competitions as informally as possible though taking care not to endanger the dogs, or the competitors.

If you are interested in finding out more about this sport, your first port of call should be your local training club. Flyball is still quite an unusual activity and few clubs may be involved with it. The clubs most likely to be involved in Flyball will be those clubs which specialise in Agility. Not all clubs will have the equipment necessary to organise Flyball training, or to schedule competitions. However, clubs are encouraged to share equipment, so if your club doesn't have a Flyball box you could always take the initiative of phoning round other clubs in your area to see if anyone is willing to share.

Equipment

There are 4 pieces of equipment required for Flyball.

Hurdles

The hurdles should be 12ins high for all classes and all sizes of dog and be painted white. For safety, the top rail must be flexible or padded.

Flyball box

The Kennel Club has an approved design for a Flyball box which has been drawn up with the safety of the competing dogs in mind.

Backstop Board

There has to be a Backstop Board in place as dogs can really hurtle over the course and there has to be something there to slow them down if they over-shoot their mark!

Balls

The balls loaded into the box must be un-punctured tennis balls. There is a risk that dogs could choke on something smaller, or hurt themselves with something larger.

Flyball – there's a catch in it!

Teams

The composition and size of teams is left to the discretion of the event organisers. Flyball can be for single competitors, or for teams of several dogs, and the organisers can decide whether substitutes are allowed or not. However many dogs there are in each team there must be someone to load the Flyball box with balls and handlers for the dogs.

The only stipulations about the compositions of teams is that they must be declared before each race and if a particular club or organisation is running several teams, dogs cannot be switched from one team to another.

Air raid!

The flyball box is padded to prevent dogs injuring themselves in their enthusiasm to catch the ball.

Judges and Stewards

The judge has overall responsibility for the competition and will control both the start and the finish. If the judge thinks that the Flyball box has malfunctioned during a race, he will stop the race and organise a re-run.

Several stewards assist the judge and they will be positioned around the course to make sure that the rules are adhered to. A steward will be on the start/finish line to ensure that a dog will only start its run when its team mate crosses the start/finish line with any part of its body. Two further stewards must be appointed to see that the hurdles and boxes are negotiated correctly.

Remember that most clubs are very happy to receive offers of help, so if you would like to try stewarding at a Flyball contest just let the event organiser know.

Competing

All competing dogs must wear a smooth, buckled collar, with which the handler will restrain the dog before the start of the race, or their turn to run. Handlers are not permitted to hold their dogs by the scruff of their necks, or in any other way.

Once the teams are assembled the judge will start the race by blowing a whistle, or similarly indicating that the race has started. At the beginning of the race the handlers must take care that their feet do not cross the start/finish line as this could result in their dog having to run again. This is not applied if a handler is resetting a jump or retrieving a loose ball.

Each dog must jump the four hurdles in succession. If it does not attempt every hurdle the steward will indicate that the dog will have to run again after the last team member

has run. If a hurdle is knocked over the dog will not be penalised as long as the dog has made a fair attempt to get over the obstacle.

When the dog reaches the box it must activate the pedal to release the ball. Box loaders may give verbal encouragement to the dogs but they are not permitted to guide, or assist, the dogs. If a dog fails to trigger the box it must run again after the other team members have run.

When the dog catches the ball it must race back, with the ball in its mouth, clearing all the hurdles again. The second dog can run as soon as the first dog crosses the start/finish line.

The dogs usually manage to race down the course, catch the ball, and return to the start/finish line in seconds! Occasionally balls are missed, or go astray but this only adds to the fun.

It's obvious that dogs love this sport – just try to stop them!

Working Trials

Will team-work and training make you and your dog work wonders?

What are Working Trials?

Dogs have been man's best friend for literally thousands of years. Many breeds were developed with specific working roles in mind; shepherding, herding, guarding, hunting and retrieving. Today many dogs still work alongside man, helping us in all sorts of areas; in the police and military; sheep and cattle herding; search and rescue organisations; guarding and patrolling properties; hunting and tracking.

Working Trials developed to test the working ability of dogs in some of these traditional roles and date back to 1924, when the Associated Sheep, Police and Army Dog Society held the very first event.

Working Trials are quite a specialist area with a small, but dedicated, following. The competitions are great fun for all those involved and, as they always take place in the country, they can be great days out in the countryside for your whole family to enjoy. You don't have to have a specialist background to enjoy, and compete in, this exciting and enthralling sport which attracts all sorts of people and many different breeds. As the competitions are designed to test working ability, they can also be very popular with dog handlers from the police and armed forces, as well as pet owners.

As in the sports of Obedience and Agility, you and your dog will have to do plenty of training together before you can begin to compete and your dog is unlikely to be ready for competition until he is about one and a half years old. All the hard work will be worth while as you will be rewarded by seeing your dog use his inherent ability to develop into a skilled working dog, and you and your dog will become a real team.

What's Involved?

Working Trials include elements used in Obedience and Agility but also have other exercises designed to test your dog's working ability. There are 5 levels of competition known as 'Stakes'.

- Companion Dog (CD) Stake
- Utility Dog (UD) Stake
- Working Dog (WD) Stake
- Tracking Dog (TD) Stake
- Patrol Dog (PD) Stake

Each Stake combines exercises in 3 sections: Control, Agility and Nosework.

The judge allocates points for each exercise completed. The marks apportioned to each exercise vary from stake to stake. A full list of the marks for each exercise within the stake are listed in The Kennel Club Rules and Regulations.

Control

Heel Work

Both on and off the lead, your dog should keep its shoulder reasonably close to your left knee whilst you walk smartly in a natural manner. The judge may ask you to vary your speed and to go through turns as well as going amongst, and around, persons and obstacles.

Pace-makers! Your dog should keep his head close to your left knee during heel work tests.

Recall to Handler

The judge will tell you to put you dog in a 'Down' or 'Sit' position and will direct you a reasonable distance away from the dog. When the judge gives the command you should recall your dog which should return at a smart pace and sit in front of you. At another command from the judge or steward your dog should go smartly to heel on your command or signal.

Sendaway and Directional Control

The judge will ask you to send your dog a set distance (the minimum distance is 20 yards). When your dog has reached the spot designated by the judge you should stop your dog in either the stand, sit or down position. At higher stakes you will be asked to re-direct your dog through a number of manoeuvres.

Sit and Down Stays

All the competitors in one stake will be judged together for the stay exercises. For the sit stay the judge or steward will say the words, ' Last Command' and you should give your final instruction for your dog to sit and stay. You should then walk to a position indicated by the judge or steward and your dog should stay perfectly still for 2 minutes until ordered to return to you. In the down stay, having given the 'Last Command' to lie down and stay, all handlers must leave and remain out of sight for 10 minutes. Your dog should not move until ordered to return to you.

Concentration is the key during Sendaway and Directional Control

Retrieve a Dumb-bell
Upon a command from the Judge, you will throw a dumb-bell, which your dog should then retrieve.

Steadiness to Gunshot
This is tested in open country. You will be warned when the test is about to take place and your dog should be walking to heel, or, free but within controlling distance. The Judge will penalise you if your dog barks, or shows any sign of fear, or aggression.

Speak on Command
This exercise appears only in the TD and PD Stakes and requires your dog to 'speak' or bark, on your command.

The test for steadiness to gunshot checks your dog's courage and his trust in you, his handler. Retrieving a dumb-bell is a more straightforward test of your dog's obedience, but no less important if you wish to succeed in Working Trials.

The three Agility obstacles are a test of your dog's fitness and training, which could lead him to scale new heights of achievement.

Agility
Clear Jump
Your dog will have to jump a 3ft hurdle. In the lower stakes, the height of the agility equipment is reduced for smaller breeds of dogs.

Long Jump
Your dog must clear a series of jumps, making up a distance of 9ft.

Scale
The scale is a vertical wall of wooden planks that your dog must scramble over. The top part of the scale may have evenly spaced wooden slats to help your dog get a footing in scaling the obstacle. You will be asked to stop 9ft in front of the wall and then send your dog to scale the wall. Having scaled the wall, your dog should remain in the stand, sit or down position before you recall him back over the scale.

Nosework
Elementary Search
Depending on which stake you have entered, an area of 15 or 25 square yards will be marked out with poles. You must send your dog into the area and order your dog to search the ground and retrieve a number of articles placed there before the start of the exercise. You will earn points for each article retrieved as well as points for overall control and style. The articles will have been handled by a search steward and will be found by your dog's scenting ability.

Track
The track is the route taken by a person unknown to the dog about to compete, across an area of ground. The track is approximately half a mile long and may include turns. Your dog should follow the route taken by the track layer some hours before, as closely as possible. A number of articles are also placed along the track which your dog should locate.

The judge will allocate marks for how closely your dog follows the route taken by the tracklayer and for each article located.

Manwork
    In the PD Stake, a number of exercises are also included which test the working skills of a patrol dog, such as pursuing and detention of 'criminals'.

A dog's scenting ability can be quite awesome to see in action. The Search and Track will test your dog's talent over different terrain and conditions.

How to Find Out More

If this intriguing sport appeals, you should contact your local training club, or a specialist Working Trials society. The Kennel Club will be able to provide details of your nearest club and tell you who to contact. Working Trials societies provide training and advice on the sport as well as organising competitions. Joining a Working Trials society will provide a valuable opportunity to learn from the experts and to expand your knowledge, as well as enjoying the social aspects of club membership!

Working Trials societies may also be able to put you in touch with experts who are willing to train you and your dog on a one to one basis. If you are going to consider this option you should try to find a suitable training ground with sufficient space to do tracking and nosework exercises. A competition track requires approximately 10 acres.

You should also consider attending The Kennel Club Working Trials Championships as a spectator. Top winning Working Trial dogs in the PD and TD Stakes qualify during the course of the year to compete in this prestigious competition which is the Working Trials equivalent of Crufts. The Championships provide a great opportunity to see the top dogs in the country in action and to talk to, and ask advice of, people involved in the sport

Competitions may be advertised at your local club. This is a good place to start as more experienced people will be on hand at the club to tell you whether you and your dog are up to standard before competing.

There are other ways of finding out what's on, when and where. The Kennel Gazette contains a Show Guide which lists the details of all the up and coming events and there are two weekly newspapers called 'Dog World' and 'Our Dogs', which can be ordered through newsagents, which also carry details. There is also a specialist Working Trials magazine, 'Working Trials Monthly' which will tell you about forthcoming events and gives you all the news and views from the Working Trials world. As The Kennel Club licenses every dog show, the Show Diary Section at The Kennel Club's offices can also tell you what competitions are scheduled to take place.

As Working Trials need a large working area they are held in the country, so can only be held when people and dogs will not damage crops. The sport of Working Trials relies on the generosity of landowners to provide enough space for the sport to thrive. Whether training, or competing, with your dog you should always respect the countryside and ensure that you do not stray onto private land without permission.

The Kennel Club tries to ensure that clubs do not hold competitions in the same area on the same day, so that there is a choice of competitions spread throughout the country.

Types of Working Trials
There are 4 different types of Working Trials competitions:

Matches and Rallies
These are informal events held either for club members, or, between the members of two or more clubs. Attending a club match or rally will probably be your first chance to compete in a Working Trial. These are always relaxed and fun occasions and offer a great opportunity to socialise with other club members and to pick up valuable tips on training and working with your dog.

Members' Working Trials
These are limited to the members of the organising society. Wins at these competitions are not counted towards your eligibility to compete in more senior competitions.

Open Working Trials
Open to all competitors. The competition at these events is fiercer than at club events and may attract competitors from all over the country.

Championship Working Trials
These too are open to all competitors, but competitors will also have the opportunity for competing for The Kennel Club's top awards, Working Trials Certificates. Winning two Certificates entitles a dog to be known as a Working Trials Champion. With top awards on offer, the very best dogs take part at this level.

How to Enter a Working Trial
Once you have found a competition you would like to enter you must get hold of a copy of the schedule which provides all the details you need to enter the competition - when and where its being held, the judge(s) name(s) what stakes are scheduled and what date completed entry forms must be received by the competition organisers, which is referred to as the 'Closing Date'.

Schedules for Working Trial competitions are easy to follow. The front cover will have the name of the society holding the competition, what sort of Working Trial it is, the name and address of the organisers and the closing date for entries. The inside of the schedule will list The Kennel Club Rules and Regulations governing the Trial and a list of the scheduled stakes being staged.

If your club has not been given copies of schedules for a trial you want to enter you should forward a stamped addressed envelope to the club staging the event.

Pulling power! A peg is typical of the track articles your dog may have to locate

The trial's base will provide refreshments and the Southern Alsatian Training Society (SATS) made sure competitors couldn't miss the base of their recent trial with good, clear signs.

Entry Forms

When you receive your entry form you must complete it legibly and accurately. You will be asked to provide the breed of your dog and his registered name, that of his sire and dam, and his date of birth. If your dog is a cross-breed on The Kennel Club Working Trials and Obedience Register you should provide exactly the same information that appears on the Register, marking dam and sire as 'Unknown' if that is the case. If you do make a mistake in the completion of this information you may lose any awards that your dog might gain at the competition, so it is vital that you take the time to get the details correct.

You should complete other details, such as your name and address and which stake you wish to enter, clearly and legibly to avoid any problems and make sure you have enclosed the correct fee. Incorrect fees are the problem Trial organisers most frequently have to deal with.

It is also vital that you sign the entry form as it forms the contract between you and the organising society. If the dog is jointly owned, both parties should sign the entry form unless one of the parties has the express permission of the other to sign on their behalf. By signing, you are declaring that your dog is fit and healthy to take part in competition and that you will abide by Kennel Club Rules and Regulations. This is essential to the management of the trial and for the sport in general.

You should post your entry form off in plenty of time of the closing date for entries. When the trial secretary receives all the entries, a ballot will be conducted to decide the running order for the tracks. You will be notified by post what time you should report for the nosework exercises.

Your Day at a Working Trial

Working Trials can take place over a number of days, and sometimes as long as a week. They are always held in the country because of the amount of land needed for tracking in all the stakes. Working Trials are rarely held up by the weather. Weather conditions have to be severe indeed for a Working Trials manager to postpone or cancel a Trial. With this in mind you should be prepared for a long day out of doors working with your dog in muddy fields and at the mercy of the weather. Clothing and footwear is, therefore, very important.

Refreshments may be available at the trial's base, but you may well want to pack your own food and beverages. Working dogs do not tend to eat before competition, but if you are going to feed your dog, or if you are staying overnight before the Trial, remember to pack your dog's food and water bowls.

The schedule will tell you how to get to the trial's base but road maps are a must if you are to find the venue without getting lost. When you get nearer to the venue it is likely to be signposted, but do leave yourself plenty of time as it can be difficult to work out exactly which country lanes lead to the farm, or fields, a trial may be being held at.

After all, you don't want to arrive flustered and late!

When you arrive at the meeting point you should let the trials manager know that you have arrived so that you can be marked as present in the catalogue. You will have been notified before the trial when you should report for competition and competitors tend to arrive at 30 minute intervals. You will be told where the various exercises will be taking place and where the tracks have been laid. It is important that you report for your exercises in plenty of time as lateness could result in elimination. You will also be advised where you should take your dog to relieve himself (known as exercise areas).

Generally, the different elements of each stake are held in different locations so the trial may be spread out over a large number of fields. Sometimes you will be able to drive to where your stake is being judged, but more usually you will have to walk.

The lower stakes, such as CD and UD, are generally completed in one day. However, the higher stakes can take place over several days. In these stakes dogs must gain a certain percentage of points in the Track to qualify to come back for the Control and Agility sections of the stake, usually held on another day.

During the trial you are permitted to use any commands, whistles or hand signals you wish to, but the judge may warn you against making unnecessary noise. Your dog should work in a happy and natural manner and display the instinctive behaviour of a working dog.

Once your dog has worked you should go back to the base. This is a valuable opportunity for you to mingle with other competitors and add to your knowledge and understanding of the sport.

At Championship Working Trials, Working Trial Certificates will be awarded to stakes winners provided they have gained the necessary percentage of the marks available. Certificates of Merit may also be awarded at Open Trials.

A 'working' breed of dog will just love the opportunity to use his natural talents and abilities in competition and you will enjoy the chance to become involved in a great new hobby with plenty of new friends to be made.

Gundogs were bred to work and how better to keep them healthy and happy than testing their skills in the field.

Field Trials and Gundog Working Tests

What are Field Trials?

Many of our best loved breeds were traditionally developed to help man in hunting. Labrador Retrievers gathered game in the field; Cocker Spaniels flushed and retrieved game; Irish Setters ranged over the fields helping us seek out birds and rabbits for the table. A great many still help us in shooting and hunting today.

Field Trials have developed to test the working ability of gundogs in competitive conditions. Trials resemble, as closely as possible, a day's shooting in the field and dogs are expected to work with all manner of game, from rabbits and hares, to partridges and pheasants. Field Trials are very popular, attract hundreds of competitors and are still very much part of our countryside sports. If you have a love and understanding of the countryside and like to see dogs working as they were intended to, this friendly and relaxed sport may be just what you are looking for.

If you want to own a dog capable of performing at a day's shooting he should come from working stock. Some dogs which have been bred for the show scene, or simply as pets, may have lost much of their working and hunting instinct which is vital in working gundogs. You will need to be dedicated to developing your dog as a working animal as, not only will he require a lot of training, working gundogs can also be more demanding than pets, or show dogs. They need plenty of exercise off the lead and their minds need to be kept active by working in the field.

Finding out About the Sport

Before you decide whether you want to get involved with this sport you should find out as much as possible about countryside sports from a number of sources.

If your dog comes from working stock, the breeder should be able to advise you about how to start to develop your dog into a working gundog and introduce you to other people in your area with similar interests.

There are many large Game and Country Fairs held all around the country every year which are well worth attending if you want to find out more. There are usually working gundog demonstrations at these fairs and you should take the time to not only watch the displays, but talk to those people involved and ask their advice. The Kennel Club also sends a stand to some of the larger Fairs and the staff are more than happy to discuss the sport with you and help to clarify any Rules and Regulations you need help with.

There are plenty of specialist publications which are filled with articles and tips about training your gundog, and the role of the dog owner and dog in the countryside, such as 'The Shooting Times', 'Shooting Gazette' and 'The Field'. These magazines also have sporting calendars which list when and where Game and Country Fairs are being held.

The Kennel Gazette also features articles about Field Trials and gundogs as well as giving the dates of forthcoming Field Trials.

Training

If you decide that this sport is for you, you can begin the process of training. You should remember that not only your dog must be fit and healthy to do a day's work, but you should be as well. You will need to be fairly robust to be able to tramp across some of the rough terrain encountered on some country shoots!

Breeds of gundog fall into 4 categories, and the training you do must bring out the traditional working abilities for the roles each category of gundog performs in the shooting field.

- Retrievers and Irish Water Spaniels
- Sporting Spaniels other than Irish Water Spaniels
- Pointers and Setters
- Breeds which Hunt, Point and Retrieve

You should start with basic Obedience. Beginning with a course like the Good Citizen Dog Scheme and progressing to more advanced Obedience training is an excellent basis for developing a working gundog. Having mastered basic Obedience, you should then join a gundog society. The Kennel Club will be able to help you find the most suitable society near to you. Gundog societies will be able to help you with specialist Field Trial training and can suggest trainers who may be willing to train you to the gun on a one to one basis. Training a working gundog is really a sport in itself and can take many years of hard work, developing a good rapport with your dog, to create a dog capable of working in the field.

A good retrieve must be quick and direct...

...but the dummy should never be mouthed by your dog.

Gundog societies may organise members' competitions and training assessments which are designed to develop your dog's ability and help with your training technique. These are helpful as your dog should learn to work surrounded by other people and dogs as it would do out in the field. Clubs may also publish newsletters and magazines, and organise all manner of social events.

Joining a Gundog society is also the only way you will be able to enter gundog competitions. Over 600 Field Trials and many Gundog Working Tests are held every year, and they are nearly all over subscribed. Preference is always given to club members so, if you want to go into competition, you will have to join several clubs to stand a chance of getting a run.

Once you have joined a Gundog Society you should ask to attend as a guest at one or two trials, to see the standard required of dogs working in the field and also to try to pick up training tips from top handlers in competition. The majority of Field Trials are held during the autumn and winter as this is the shooting season.

Gundog Working Tests (GWTs)

Most gundogs aren't ready to work in competition for at least two years and the first sort of competition you will probably enter will be a Gundog Working Test. These competitions are for members of the organising club only . They are designed to further good, sound, gundog work and encourage dogs' natural working ability, but do not involve shooting live game. Work is done with dummies, or cold game, and these friendly competitions are a natural extension of the training you will already be doing with your dog.

There are 3 types of Gundog Working Test, designed for different breeds of dog. Whenever possible dogs should be tested at a drive, walking up and in water.

Retrievers

Retrievers are tested on their game finding ability and the quickness and directness of the retrieve.

Judges will be looking for quick pickups and fast returns, natural nose and marking ability, quietness in handling, control, drive and style.

Spaniels

A Spaniel's first task in the shooting field is to find game and flush within range of the handler. Spaniels will be judged on how well they quarter the ground, find and flush game. In retrieving shot game spaniels should pickup quickly and deliver the game cleanly to the handler. The judge will be looking for natural nose and marking ability, quickness in gathering retrieves, control, drive and style.

Breeds which Hunt, Point and Retrieve (HPR)

It is difficult to assess pointing through artificial tests and there are limitations to how this can be done in a GWT. HPR breeds will be tested and judged on their quartering, hunting and retrieving skills in similar ways to Retrievers and Spaniels.

Entering a Field Trial

When you have been a member of a Gundog society for some time and been attending training sessions and GWTs, you will generally be advised by the society secretary when your dog is ready for competition. Gundog societies send schedules to all their members before a trial and when you and your dog are ready you should complete the entry form and return it.

The schedule will tell you when and where the Trial is taking place and what stakes are scheduled. Field Trials can consist of one or more stakes, which are separate competitions at that trial and can be limited by the age or previous experience and wins of the dog. You should study the schedule carefully to ensure that you enter the correct stake for your dog. It is also important to complete the entry form as legibly and accurately as possible; your dog's registered details should be exactly as they appear on The Kennel Club registration certificate and your name and address should be clearly marked to assist the Field Trial secretary in advising competitors of the draw. The schedule will also tell you by what date your entry form should be returned to the trial organisers, known as the 'closing date'.

After the closing date for entries the society committee will conduct a draw to pick the competitors for the trial. As has already been mentioned Field Trials are usually over-subscribed so you may not be lucky enough to get a run the very first time you apply for entry. Different types of trial allow different numbers of competitors and the trial secretary will advise all entrants of their placing in the draw. If there are only 20 places available, and you are number 32, you will not get a run unless 12 people in front of you drop out. With so many people keen to compete you must advise the trial organisers immediately if you have to drop out of a trial to give another competitor chance to run in the trial.

Water performance!

A firm grasp on the situation.

Be prepared to to work in both cold and wet conditions...

Preparation

There's a great deal to think about before......

Firstly, you must dress appropriately. You should wear plenty of layers of warm clothing, and, wellington boots and a water and wind proof coat are a must. It's also important that your clothes are dark, or in neutral tones, and not brightly coloured as this may startle game. With the vagaries of the British weather you are well advised to take a change of clothing with you, so that you are not faced with a cold and damp car journey home.

You should also pack the food and drink you are going to need during the course of the day. Sometimes judges do not stop for lunch, particularly when there are reduced daylight hours in the autumn and winter, so you should think about things you can eat in the field if you cannot wait until a day's competition is over.

Field Trials usually mean a long car journey so think about your dog's needs too - a good strong travelling box and plenty of water will make his trip comfortable. Working dogs are not fed before a day's work but you should remember to pack your dog's bowls and some dog food as you may not return home from a trial until late in the evening.

Although the schedule and draw will tell you where the trial is going to take place you should also take a good map with you. Field Trials are usually signposted when you get near to the meeting point but it can often be very difficult to track down exactly which field down which country lane you need to be heading for.

Many people choose to travel the day before the trial and stay in Bed and Breakfast accommodation. If you do decide to do this, always double check that the management are happy to take dogs and that there is somewhere suitable to exercise your dog.

At the Trial

You should allow yourself plenty of time to reach the meeting point. If you are late one of the reserves may get the chance of running in your place and all your preparation and long journey will have been wasted.

Once you have found the meeting point you should let the Field Trial secretary know that you have arrived. They will mark you as present on the card, which lists all the people and dogs taking part in the trial, and give you a numbered arm band which you must wear throughout the trial and is the means by which you will be identified.

Before the trial starts, a briefing will be held to introduce the host (if present), the gamekeeper and the guns, to explain how the day will run and any special instructions. Competitors must always attend this briefing both for their own interest and to be courteous to the trial organisers and host. Field Trial societies rely on the generosity of land owners to host trials and keep the sport alive. The host not only provides the land to hold the trial and the game, but also the guns, the beaters, the game carriers and the gamekeeper. It is vital, therefore, that you treat the countryside with respect and always be courteous to the estate staff.

...luckily working dogs seldom seem to care what the weather throws at them!

After the briefing, everyone will either walk or drive to where the stakes are to take place. Safety is a very important consideration and spectators, and dogs and owners not competing, must stay behind a red flag carried by one of the stewards. This ensures that everyone stays out of the way of the guns and that people do not stray onto parts of the estate they are not meant to.

During each stake the judge(s) will ask each dog to work a number of times under various conditions. The Kennel Club's J Regulations set out the manner in which each exercise is conducted. Competitors should make themselves familiar with the Regulations well before they enter their first Field Trial. Judges will be looking closely at how your dog works, making a note of all his strengths, but also of his major faults. There are also a number of eliminating faults in each stake such as whining and barking, hard mouth, running in and chasing, failing to find game that another dog can find, and changing game whilst retrieving. There are different eliminating faults for each stake and handlers should be well aware of these both in training and in competition.

If your dog does commit an eliminating fault he is excluded from further competition at the trial. This can be very disappointing if it occurs on your dog's first run but you should lose with good grace and enjoy the rest of the day's shooting. It is considered very poor form to leave a trial early simply because your dog has not performed to the best of his ability. Always thank the judges and trial secretary before you leave.

Handling your Dog

Attending your first Field Trial may cause your dog to behave differently than he does in training. Young dogs in particular, can be bothered by crowds and if this is the case you can move a little way from other competitors and officials. You must, however, let the steward know what you are doing and why. You will not be penalised for controlling your dog in this manner. In fact, it is a good idea to tell your judge and steward that you are competing in your first Trial as they will make their directions clear and offer you help.

Working gundogs should be kept under good control at all times, both whilst waiting to compete and during the stakes. You should always be aware of how your dog is reacting and what he is doing. If he does misbehave, you should never handle your dog harshly, especially during a Trial. This could land you in trouble with The Kennel Club and also indicates that you have not trained your dog properly. All dogs should be trained and worked using plenty of encouragement.

If for any reason you become aware that your dog is not going to work well - we all have our off days - you should ask the judge's permission to withdraw. This is a courtesy that must be observed. At the end of the trial there will be a number of presentations that all competitors are expected to stay for. The host, gamekeeper and guns will be thanked; 4 awards for each stake will be presented together with any Certificates of Merit other dogs may have earned; the overall winner will thank the judges and make any other comments about the trial.

Sitting on the fence is no way to succeed at Field Trials!

The Kennel Club Junior Organisation

Kids love dogs and no-one knows this better than the KCJO who organise all sorts of events for dog-loving youngsters.

What is the K.C.J.O?

One of the great things about owning dogs is that they can bring joy to everyone, no matter how old, or, how young. Children in particular are able to have great fun training and playing with their dogs and, if you take your family along to any of the events described in this booklet, you may soon find that the most junior members of your family are keen to become more involved with the world of dogs.

Many hundreds of children attend Kennel Club licensed activities, and The Kennel Club wants as many children as possible to learn about the great benefits of dog ownership and how to develop a loving but responsible relationship with dogs. With this in mind The Kennel Club Junior Organisation (KCJO) was set up in 1985.

Goals

The KCJO has three specific and important goals.

Firstly, to encourage young people to take an interest in the care and training of dogs and to enjoy all activities connected with dogs; secondly, to promote courtesy, sportsmanship, loyalty and self discipline; and lastly, to develop a sense of responsibility in canine activities.

Youngsters between the ages of 8 and 18 can become members of The Kennel Club Junior Organisation. Once a member, an information pack will be sent out providing details of all the fun, interesting and exciting activities the new member can become involved in. Would-be members do not need to have a dog in the family - the only requirement to be a member is to have a keen interest in dogs, their care and training.

Regions

The activities of the KCJO are conducted on a regional basis with organisers appointed for 8 areas:

- North West and Isle of Man
- North East
- Midlands
- South and South West
- South East and East Anglia
- Scotland
- Wales
- Northern Ireland

The Regional Organisers form the KCJO Policy Council and set up many interesting talks and practical demonstrations to broaden members' knowledge of all aspects of dogs and dog competitions - from how to groom different breeds of dog for the Show ring, to tips on Agility training. All sorts of visits might also be organised to organisations such as Guide Dogs for the Blind, Police Dog Training Centres, Veterinary Centres and Rescue and re-homing kennels. All these activities are detailed in informative and colourful quarterly newsletters.

Competitions

As well as these regional activities, there are all sorts of events exclusively for KCJO members held at dog shows and competitions all over the country every year. Although members are encouraged to work hard to succeed in all these different activities, the fun aspect of dogs and the dog world is never forgotten and it is hoped that KCJO members always enjoy themselves.

Stakes Classes

KCJO Stakes classes are classes at Kennel Club licensed Shows limited to KCJO members. Entry in these classes lets youngsters learn all about presenting their dog for exhibition and competing with their dog in the show ring. As they will be competing against other KCJO members firm friendships are quickly developed and many members become dedicated to this hobby.

Wins in Stakes Classes can qualify youngsters to go through to the KCJO Stakes Final held at Crufts every year. This is every member's dream and competition can be quite fierce to bring home the coveted trophies.

Show Junior Handler of the Year

Each KCJO Region will hold a handling competition every year in three age groups , 8-11, 12-15, 16-18. At these competitions, members will be judged purely on how well they present and handle their dogs in the show ring. The judge will be looking for preparation and presentation, rapport with the dog, effective use of ring space, sympathetic handling and consideration and courtesy shown to other handlers in the show ring. Members must also demonstrate a sound knowledge of their breed's Breed Standard as well as why their breed of dog should be presented in the way that it is.

Youngsters can learn the art of responsible dog ownership...

...as well as taking part in competitions like the Show Junior Handler of the Year.

Winners go through to their national handling final held at Crufts every year where they undergo an assessment on the theory of dog handling, as well as competing in the final round of Show Junior Handler of the Year. The overall winner is presented with a silver salver and may also go through to represent the UK at the International Handler of the Year Competition also held at Crufts.

Obedience Tests

The KCJO is not just concerned with Dog Shows. There are also tests of members' proficiency and ability in the sport of Obedience. Kennel Club registered Training Clubs, KCJO Events and Kennel Club licensed events can all schedule tests of Obedience for KCJO members. The exercises in these classes are similar to the exercises found in the sport of Obedience proper. Those members gaining the correct qualifying marks are rewarded with merit badges and certificates. Each region sends a team to the Crufts final.

Points gained through these KCJO classes and through normal Obedience competitions count towards entry to an annual Obedience Competition. Winners are presented with a trophy at Crufts.

Agility Competitions

Members win points towards Agility merit badges and certificates by competing at Kennel Club licensed Agility events during the course of a year.

Junior Agility also has its climax at Crufts with the KCJO Agility Dog of the Year. Winners of Agility Certificates that year all compete at a Qualifying Final and the first four in all age groups go through to the final at Crufts.

Will you and your dog make it to 'pole position' at the Crufts Agility Final?

Junior of the Year

The highest award for a member is to become Junior of the Year and win the Shaun McAlpine Memorial Trophy which is awarded in a ceremony at Crufts every year. Members must prepare a project and keep a log book of all their activities throughout the year connected with dogs. This isn't just about showing or handling dogs, or a list of shows attended and wins gained - it embraces all canine disciplines and to win members must show a real commitment to the world of dogs. Perhaps members help at kennels, rescue stalls, steward at dogs shows, or take part in sponsored events. All of these can contribute to making a Junior of the Year in the eyes of the Judges whether the member owns a dog or not.

Quiz

A number of quizzes about dogs and canine matters are held at KCJO events throughout the year. From the best performances, Regional Teams are selected for an Inter-Regional Knock-out competition and a Final is held each year to find the winning region.

Proficiency Badges

The KCJO awards badges of merit for members passing tests in Showing, Handling, Agility, Obedience and Advanced Obedience. There are also merit badges for becoming Junior of the Year and for members qualifying for their Regional Quiz Team.

National Camp

A National Camp is held in the summer of every year. All KCJO members have the chance to attend and learn about many aspects of dogs and dog competitions as well as having great fun with all their friends. This is a real high spot in the KCJO year and a firm favourite with the youngsters. Unfortunately, its great popularity means that numbers sometimes have to be limited.

Triathlon and Biathlon

These competitions test Juniors' ability in Breed, Obedience and Agility for the Triathlon and just Obedience and Agility for the Biathlon. They are held at KCJO events and the winners are the members gaining most points in all or both disciplines. These events can be great fun and give Juniors the chance to enjoy another different level of competition.

Stewarding

The KCJO Council is often approached by show secretaries requesting members who would be available to act as ring stewards. With this in mind the KCJO devised guidelines for juniors to learn about stewarding at dog shows, obedience tests and agility competitions. Merit badges and certificates are awarded to Juniors who have worked as 'apprentices' at the required numbers of shows and competitions.

To join this interesting organisation and to take part in all of these fun activities contact The Kennel Club on 0870 6066750, ext 230 for an application form.

Why not enjoy a real bow-wow pow-wow at the KCJO camp – there's so much to learn and friends to be made.

Problem Solving

Dog shows and competitions are highly enjoyable but, unfortunately, you are bound to run into some sort of problem one day. Luckily the show or competition management will be on hand to help.

Competition Management

Each canine sport has different officials in charge of organising and running each competition. For dog shows the Show Secretary and/or Show Manager will be in charge; in Obedience competitions it is the Society Secretary and/or Chief Steward; at Working Trials the Working Trial Manager; at Agility Tests the Show Manager; at Field Trials the Field Trial Manager. Whatever the title of the competition organiser you should head for the organiser if you encounter any sort of problem on the day of the competition.

It can be a pretty hectic time running a show, but if you need help, or have some constructive criticism, organisers will always make time to see you.

If the benching is broken, or unsuitable, the organiser will be able to, either have someone from the benching company sort out the problem, or, find you an alternative bench. If you are entered in the wrong class in the catalogue, the organisers will look at your entry form to find out where the problem has arisen and transfer you to another class if appropriate. If you've lost some property or want to know what time Best in Show is going to be judged, call in at the organisers' office.

If you have a complaint about any of the arrangements for the competition you should raise it with the organisers. After all, the organisers cannot improve the event if they are not provided with any feedback about where competitors may think they have gone wrong.

Queries

Competition organisers can also help you with the clarification of The Kennel Club Rules and Regulations. If you have not understood why something has happened in competition, the organisers will always respond to polite requests for explanations of the Rules and Regulations. Remember though, that officials may be very busy organising the competition, so don't raise queries if they are in the middle of dealing with something else.

Objections

Although it rarely happens, occasionally an exhibitor, or competitor, will contravene Kennel Club Regulations. They may enter a dog in a class or stake for which it is not eligible, their dog may be aggressive or even bite someone, or they may question the judge's decision. All these things should be reported to the organiser straight away.

If you think there has been a breach of Kennel Club Regulations, or you have encountered any sort of serious problem, you should seek the advice of the organisers. They will be able to help you either sort the problem out, or guide you through the procedure of lodging a formal objection, to be adjudicated on by The Kennel Club after the competition. You may be asked to pay a (usually refundable) fee to lodge the objection and you will have to write an account of the

problem in the 'Incident Book'. It is rare that this step is taken as most dog competitors never have to become involved in making formal complaints to The Kennel Club, or encounter serious problems.

Veterinary Attention

Every competition, either has to have a Veterinary Surgeon in attendance, or has to have made arrangements for one to be on call. If your dog should become ill on the way to an event, becomes unwell at the competition itself , or it has an accident, you should go straight to the organisers to seek assistance.

Weather

Outdoor dog Shows can be plagued with weather problems. A heavy downpour of rain can disrupt judging, but outdoor Shows must always have alternative judging rings to keep interruptions to a minimum. If it does rain the steward will direct all the exhibitors to the 'wet weather accommodation', as it is known, and judging should recommence as soon as possible.

The other canine disciplines of Obedience, Agility, Flyball, Working Trials and Field Trials tend to go on whatever the weather. Judges and stewards do, however, have to ensure that dogs, competitors and spectators are not put in any danger, and in very severe conditions can abandon a competition.

Hot weather can also cause problems. Many of the breeds with thick coats, like Chow Chows, can become very uncomfortable on sunny days and you should remember

It's not just the rain that can cause problems at shows – heavy-coated breeds can really suffer in the heat of the sun, so keep them in the shade.

that, whatever breed you have, your dog will need plenty of water, and spells in the shade, if it's a hot day. Often, the 'wet weather accommodation' at Shows may be used on very hot days so that judging can carry on in the shade.

Never, under any circumstances, leave your dog in a car on a hot day. All responsible dog owners know that dogs are at great risk of over-heating and dehydration if left in these conditions. If you do leave your dog in the car, you will be asked by the show management to attend to your dog straight away and you will be reported to The Kennel Club for possible disciplinary procedures against you. Always put the care of your dog first.

Do's and Don'ts

The Kennel Club Yearbook contains all the Rules and Regulations that govern Dog Shows, Obedience Competitions, Agility Tests, Flyball Competitions, Working Trials, Field Trials and Gundog Working Tests and although you do not need to know all of them before you enter a competition, there are some things that everyone needs to be aware of.

- All dogs must be registered with The Kennel Club if they are to take part in a Kennel Club licensed event (except Exemption Dog Shows).

- You should only enter Kennel Club licensed events.

- No dog under 6 months of age is eligible for any form of competition. No dog under 18 months of age may enter Agility, Flyball and Working Trial competitions.

- No bitches in season should be brought to Obedience, Agility, Flyball, Working Trial or Field Trial Competitions.

- No bitches may be mated within the precincts of a show or competition.

- You should not allow your dog to foul anywhere other than the allotted 'exercise areas' and always clean up after your dog.

- You should always leave show grounds and venues clean and tidy.

- It simply is not acceptable that a dog displays aggression in competition. If your dog growls, or otherwise shows aggression, the judge will immediately exclude the dog from the ring, and from further competition. If your dog does not like being handled by the judge, or competing, then perhaps you really shouldn't be taking your dog to competitions, and certainly you should look at taking your dog to training classes.

**The KC Yearbook...
for the full picture.**

- The Kennel Club expects all people taking part in its licensed events to conduct themselves in a sportsmanlike manner. You should never interfere with another dog in competition, or try to distract a dog, or otherwise impede him from giving his best.

- You should never handle your dog harshly, or use punitive correction at a competition. To do so will land you in trouble with The Kennel Club and demonstrates that you have not trained your dog properly.

- Your dog should be kept on a lead and under good control at all times at a competition (except when safely back at his bench at benched shows). Again, safety is paramount, and all responsible dog owners want to enjoy a good day out without problems of loose, or unruly, dogs.

- You should never question the decision of the judge. You have entered the show to get that judge's opinion of your dog and if he doesn't like your dog you should simply make up your mind not to show or compete under him or her again. Loud complaints and arguments will only land you in trouble with The Kennel Club so if you lose do so with a good grace.

- If your dog has an operation you must write to The Kennel Club to seek permission to continue to show your dog. As The Kennel Club keeps the Register of pure-bred dogs in this country it needs to know that the dogs being exhibited at shows are the best examples of the breed and haven't been surgically altered to improve their chances of winning.

The judge will always be happy to discuss the merits of your dog, but remember – never question his choice of winners or decisions.

More Great Dog Days Out!

There are many other activities which you can enjoy with your dog. Here are just a few to think about.

Have dog – will travel!

Exemption Dog Shows

Although the best way to become involved in the world of dogs is to join a club and to attend basic obedience classes, many people's first encounter with the world of dogs comes through attending a 'dog show' as part of a charity open day, or at a fete. These are known as Exemption dog shows as they are exempt from many of The Kennel Club's Rules and Regulations governing competitions and dogs which are not registered with The Kennel Club may take part. These competitions are great fun and very relaxed events.

There may be some 'breed' classes, such as a class for Gundogs, or a class for Terriers, and there will also be plenty of classes with imaginative titles like ' Dog which looks most like its owner', or, 'Dog with the waggiest tail'. With classes like these you can see that these definitely are fun competitions!

Basic Obedience classes may also be scheduled though none of the other canine disciplines.

Look out for shows like this being advertised locally, as going to an Exemption dog show may be your first taste of competition with your dog and, once you are hooked, you may decide that you want to go on to bigger and better things!

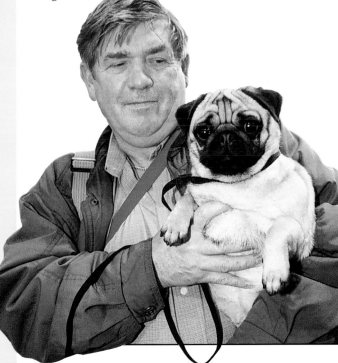

Exemption shows hold all sorts of classes – which one will these two go for?

Why not include your dog in your hobbies? Even line-dancing with dogs has been given a whirl!

Tripping the light fantastic!

Heelwork to Music

This hobby is only just starting to gain popularity in this country. It was started in the USA and can now be seen at exhibitions like Discover Dogs. Handlers have to train closely with their dogs to achieve a closely co-ordinated and artistic display of teamwork set to music which compliments their style. This hobby will appeal to people already interested in Obedience work.

PAT Dogs

As well as making great companions, many studies have shown that dogs and cats can benefit our health too. They help to lower our blood pressure and they keep us fit and healthy. The charity, Pets as Therapy have discovered that people in hospital can make real gains simply by having the chance to see, stroke and play with dogs. If you think your dog is gentle and steady enough to undertake this rewarding work why not contact Pets as Therapy to find out more on 01732 848499.

Rescue Kennels Volunteers

Television programmes like Animal Hospital and Pet Rescue alert us to the many animals that are abandoned, or need re-homing, each year. Whether you own a dog or not you might want to consider offering your help to your local rescue organisation. They usually need help to walk dogs and to feed all the animals in their care and are grateful for any offers of help. Perhaps you've got some bright ideas for fund-raising? Why not volunteer to help out at open days? However you get involved you will be sure to gain a lot in helping the animals that need you the most

The dog world has something for everyone – whether you fancy attempting a world record attempt at a 60 pole weave, or going hot on the trail with your Bloodhound!

Bloodhound Trials

Everyone has seen pictures of Bloodhounds relentlessly following a scent to track down a missing person or a lost possession. If you own a Bloodhound, you may wish to consider competing in a Kennel Club Bloodhound Trial where your dog's tracking ability is tested in competition conditions. To find out more contact The Bloodhound Club, or the Association of Bloodhound Breeders. The Kennel Club can supply you with up to date contact details for these clubs.

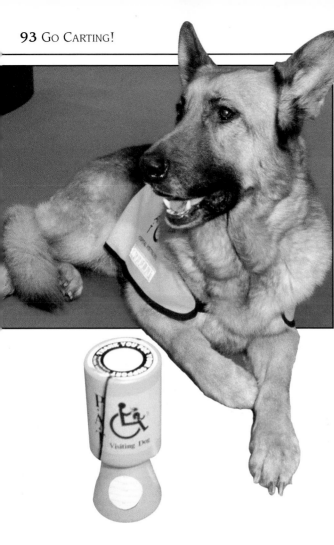

If you don't have a dog, why not help out at you local rescue kennels – then you'll have plenty to care for!

Snow – mobiles!

Bernese Mountain Dog Carting

Bernese Mountain Dogs were originally bred to carry small loads in the mountains. Many picture postcards and paintings portray these beautiful animals harnessed with small carts delivering milk and the like. If you have a Bernese Mountain Dog, your breed club will be able to tell you all about this breed's fascinating history and put you in touch with people who organise demonstrations of the breed's traditional role at exhibitions such as Crufts.

Siberian Husky Sledding

There is a thriving interest in dog sledding in this country. Siberian Huskies were originally bred to pull sledges in the arctic north and there are several clubs who still organise races to tests their dogs' working ability in this traditional role. For further details contact Siberian Husky breed clubs. The Kennel Club can provide contact details.